I Am Not Contagious

A Young Woman's Journey through

the Darkness of Colon Cancer and Parkinson's Disease

into the Light of Hope

By Allison Smith-Conway

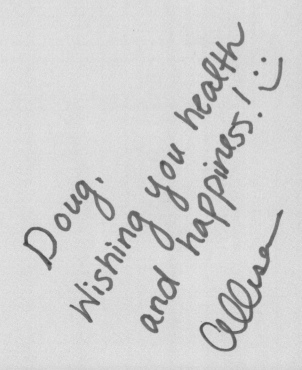

Doug,
Wishing you health
and happiness! :)

Allison

AuthorHouse™
1663 Liberty Drive
Bloomington, IN 47403
www.authorhouse.com
Phone: 1-800-839-8640

Published by AuthorHouse 02/11/2012

ISBN: 978-1-4685-4905-8 (sc)

Library of Congress Control Number: 2012902727

Any people depicted in stock imagery provided by Thinkstock are models,
and such images are being used for illustrative purposes only.
Certain stock imagery © Thinkstock.

This book is printed on acid-free paper.

authorHOUSE®

Dedication

This book is dedicated to my parents, who gave me life,

And to my husband, who gave me hope.

I Am Not Contagious

Acknowledgements

Where do I begin? I did not have a clue how difficult writing this book would be. It was not the mechanics of putting everything on paper, but the horrific process of reliving my darkest moments. As I was deep in the process, I began to see how therapeutic it was for me, and it gave me the awesome opportunity to see how many people have supported and loved me during this unreal adventure we call life. This book would have not been possible without the help of these wonderful people.

- *Ariela Wilcox at The Wilcox Agency, for reading 500 words in a newspaper and then believing in my potential to write this memoir. (wilcoxagency@sbcglobal.net)*

- *David Davis at MDC Advertising and Design, for encouraging my creativity to evolve. (david@mcd-adv.com)*

- *Dr. Christopher Duma, who not only gave me a new lease on life, but also took a chance a girl with a crazy dream.*

- *Dr. Kenneth Martinez, Dr. Scott Martin and all my friends at the practice. I am honored to be a part of an amazing team.*

- *Heidi Cortese who did my first television interview and has remained my cheerleader ever since.*

- *Dr. Lisa Abaid, Dr. Andrew Siskind, Dr. David Kauffman, and all my unbelievable physicians who have been trying to figure me out for years.*

- *Medtronics, not only did you create the stimulator that controls my Parkinson's, your team has been unbelievable supportive and kind.*

- *Alison Reynard, you showed me the power of yoga and friendship.*

- *Dr. Stuart Melcer, you saved my life, literally.*

- *Michelle Lund, you are the definition of a true friend, and I am grateful to have you in my life.*

- *Casie Sullivan, you have been in my corner from the start, and I am honored to have you as my friend.*

- *Dr. Richard Landis, thank you for being so patient with our journey.*

- *Claudia Schou, you have encouraged my growth and are always up for a challenge.*

- *Justin Saunders, you've got my back! Every hero needs a sidekick.*

- *Lindsay Susskind, my partner in crime, I am so happy this experience has brought us together.*

- *Babs Dempsey and Cindy Miller, for joining the cause; with your help we have been able to expand our reach.*

- *Barbara Filippone, my mentor, my friend.*

- *Davis Phinney, you inspire me to keep looking for moments of victory, every day.*

- *Michael J. Fox, words fall short. Thank you for paving the road that I am traveling.*

- *National Parkinson's Foundation Orange County Chapter and American Parkinson's Disease Association, for your continual support in the community.*

- *Beverly Simpson, for accepting me into your family with open arms, love you!*

- *Sharon and Jerry Miller, for cheering me on, regardless of the politics involved.*

- *PM Howard, "I am smiling, I have Parkinson's." You are extremely talented and always willing to help. A good man to have on my team!*

- *Casey and Anthony Klein, you were there from the start. Thank you for your unconditional love. Casey, I miss seeing you every day in our condo.*

- *Brenda and Kenny Rowland, for celebrating my gutter balls.*

- *All the members that support my Parkinson's in Balance program, thank you for your enduring devotion. You are all heroes in my eyes.*

- *Patrick LoSasso, you have the drive and knowledge to help our community. Thank you for including me in the evolution of your Brain Ball Fx.*

Most importantly, this book would have not been possible without the love, encouragement and support of my family and friends. Thank you for keeping me strong.

- My husband, Jason you are my rock. Thank you for loving me.

- Mom and Dad, through pain, happiness and everything in between, you have always been there for me. I love you.

- Todd and Beth Smith, "maybe your intestine and my kidney can come together to create a superior being to rule the world." It is a disgusting thought, but thanks for the laughs! Beth, for always checking up on me, I finally have a sister.

Chapter 1:   My Normal Childhood   3

Chapter 2:   Lucky Number 13   11

Chapter 3:   The best years of my life?   19

Chapter 4:   In the Beginning   27

Chapter 5:   May 5th, 2003   39

Chapter 6:   Embracing the Madness   47

Chapter 7:   Dating and Disease   55

Chapter 8:   Life, Love and Parkinson's   67

Chapter 9:   Call me Sparkie the Parkie   73

Chapter 10:   Strength in Pain   87

Chapter 11:   Parkinson's in Balance   95

Epilogue: A happy ending on a roller coaster   105

Photos: Memories from my Journey   114

I Am Not Contagious

Foreword

By Christopher Duma, MD, FACS

When Allison Conway walked into my office with the diagnosis of Parkinson's Disease, she was beaming with life and energy. Just like many patients, she sat opposite me, twitching and writhing with dyskinesia (a side effect of her medication). But there was one thing special about Allison, she was only 32. She is part of a subset of Parkinson's patients we call "YOPPIES" – young onset Parkinson's patient. She had come to my office to see what options of treatment were available to her because the thought of a 9-year course to complete disability was not what she signed up for.

You see, I am one of a few neurosurgeons who pioneered the implantation of pacemakers into the brain, a technology that is exactly equivalent to a heart pacemaker except the wires go to the brain instead of the heart. DBS, or "deep brain stimulation," was approved by the FDA in 1997, and I've been implanting them ever since. Allison came to me with hope that she could have a chance for a normal life; a chance at a future.

Allison was impetuous as she made this decision only a month into her diagnosis having realized that she had been symptomatic for at least three years prior. She was unwilling to go the usual course which would be at least 5 to 7 more years of medication changes; taking this medication sometimes hourly, putting up with side effects of drowsiness, balance problems and cognitive changes ever worsening over that period of time. She could not wait. She is not the type to sit around idly and wait for her medications to "kick in." She's a doer, she's a go-getter. Surgeons have the same mentality: we require instant gratification. We enjoy the quick fix and relish in the artistry of our work. We can't wait. I could relate.

In medical school we are taught not to internalize or personalize our patients' problems. It could be too "overwhelming" for us. This is not my case. I'm an empath. I put myself into every one of my patient's shoes and scratch out a plan for them that I would use upon myself or my loved ones. Can I blame this young lady for taking her fate into her own hands? Not at all. It is exactly what I would have done in her shoes.

As I sat with Allison and discussed her current problem, things got even worse. The story of her battle with colon cancer unfolded and I marveled at what a bad hand of cards this young lady had been dealt. She had undergone a multitude of medical operations on her abdomen to battle this disease and beat it only to be diagnosed with Parkinson's disease a few years later. As she relayed this history to me she had that "yeah, I know, I've got another impossible disease to cure" look about her. She was resolute, firm with her conviction, and ready to go. So was I.

My average Parkinson's patient is usually 60 or 70 years old carrying that diagnosis for at least 9 or 10 years. The neurologists' standard of care is to medicate patients over all these years, requiring increasing dosage of their medication with less and less success to the point where the patient may finally be sent to the neurosurgeon for surgical management. The surgical management of certain symptoms related to Parkinson's disease dates back to the 1940s and '50s. At that time, in order to rid a patient of a tremor or the stiffness and rigidity of Parkinsonism, we used to burn areas of the brain with a small probe heated to 180°F. As one might imagine if the wrong area were burned, the damage could not be undone.

In 1997, the FDA approved a "new" procedure where instead of destroying an area of the brain the surgeon could place an electrode precisely in the area of the brain, attached to a simulator, to stop a tremor or the stiffness of Parkinson's Disease. This procedure was invented by a French neurosurgeon in 1990. The advantages were obvious. No areas of brain were destroyed, and various stimulation parameters could be adjusted after the procedure at a later date, at the patient's bedside, via a programmer that acts telemetrically through the patient's skin.

Soon the neurologists were referring patients to me for this procedure. However they were often extremely elderly at that point, had had the disease for greater than 15 or 20 years, and were at the end stages of its natural history. These patients were felt to be "lost hopes" in the neurologists eyes. But we started valiantly with this patient population. As time went on the neurosurgeons were demanding healthier patients; patients who were not so advanced in their disease process and who had truly reached their limits of medical therapy. Over the ensuing years we began to see younger and younger patients. Allison is one of them. Her story is exactly that - one of perseverance, hope and sheer guts.

Preface

I was having a hard time sleeping in my empty bed. The mattress felt like it stretched a mile in length, adding to the misery of being alone. My 400 thread count periwinkle sheets had cheerful white flowers embroidered in an orderly fashion. It was almost comical that just a month ago, I spent hours at "Bed, Bath and Beyond" trying to decide which brand, pattern and thread count I should purchase. But now looking down at the sheets, all I could see were blurry white circles. I tried to focus my eyes on something that looked familiar, but I could only focus on the bright glow of the clock.

It was 4:47am. The pain medication was wearing off, and the sting of a six inch incision on my tummy was becoming unbearable. With a deep breath, I slowly rolled off of my bed and onto my feet. My body felt heavy as I shuffled down the hallway to the living room. I slowly lowered myself onto the couch, gripping my childhood blanket. A small tangled ball of fabric, which I called *"blue blankin"* always brought comfort to me, even though on multiple occasions, it was mistaken for a cleaning rag or a torn t-shirt that needed to be taken to the garbage. Just before my body had found the sofa, a sharp pain punched me in the stomach; it felt as if someone had stabbed me with a hot metal iron. I grabbed my stomach and gasped.

I lifted my shirt and looked at my swollen stomach. It wasn't a dream. The incision caked with dried blood brought me into that reality. At the end of my stitches there was a plastic bag attached to my body. Like a parasite living off of its host, it gripped onto my flesh. At age 24, I had a colostomy bag. I had just gotten home to Tucson, Arizona after enduring an inter-state journey to have my diseased colon removed.

I heard movement in the other room, and soon I saw my mom coming down the hallway. She had been diligently by my side through the emotional cyclone of the previous week. In an oversized t-shirt and messy hair, she stood in front of me. As we stood in silence, the weak glow of sunlight began creeping into the room. There was nothing to say. We just looked at each other and began to sob. She came to me and hugged me, as tears were burning my eyes.

I had just survived my first surgery for colon cancer. Maybe I was being naive, but I desperately wanted to believe the hardest part was over, I just had to heal and then everything would go back to being normal like when I was a kid. Thankfully I had no way to predict that the next three years of my life would include 14 surgical procedures, over 30 hospital visits, nearly dying twice, and the slow dissolution of my marriage.

Chapter 1:
My Normal Childhood

Only a couple years old, but I am not afraid to get in the dirt.

I guess the best way to tell you about my life would be to start from the beginning. I grew up in Colorado which was a dream for any little girl; beautiful seasons, huge bedroom full of toys, great friends, and loving parents. My parents let me have just enough room to make my own mistakes and learn from them, but they were careful to make sure I did not get hurt. I was in third grade when I learned my first hard lesson. My home was within walking distance from my elementary school, which made for a nice stroll on a warm day in May. I had the same routine of mundane activities that I partook in each day. Get up, brush my teeth, eat breakfast, style my blonde locks in the latest 1980's hairdo then walk to school.

I would sit in an incredibly uncomfortable chair for 7 hours. You know, the type of desk that is welded onto a plastic chair. I would pretend that I was paying attention to the teacher's lesson until the school bell rang, and then I ran home before my parents got done with work so I could sneak sugary treats before supper. As a family, we would have dinner, which was prepared by my mother and then watch prime time television, which usually included "Family Ties" and "Cheers". I had to be ready and in my twin size canopy bed by 9 pm so my Dad could do the "tuck game" where he would tuck the corners of my sheets all around me until I was stuffed like a burrito and could not move. I do think this was a ploy to keep me in bed at night, but I played along with it anyway. We would say our goodnights and go to sleep, then the day started all over again.

My Dad has this amazing quality of being strong and sensitive. He is a perfect combination of flannel and testosterone with an empathetic tone. When I would have a bad day at school or I was upset about something, my Dad would take the time to come and talk to me at night. After he would tuck me in, he would brush my hair with his hand and explain to me how everything would get better. He has strong morals and raised my brother and I to treat people with respect. I felt safe with my Dad, like nothing could ever hurt me.

One day I was on a swing at my school's playground waiting for the 1ˢᵗ bell to ring. My best friend Jenny walked up to me and sat down on the swing next to me. "I hate school" she mumbled as she dragged her feet across the ground. "I know. I do too, it is so boring!" I replied. Jenny's eyes lit up as she excitedly said "I have a super fun game we can play, it's called 'Hokey'." Now yes, maybe I should have been a little suspicious but I asked her to tell me about this awesome game. "All we have to do is leave school and go back to my house. We can watch T.V., play games, and I have left over pizza we can eat?" she stated. This game sounded amazing and, to tell you the truth, it was the pizza that sold me on the idea.

Jenny and I left school and started on our new adventure. As we strolled down the neighborhood streets, we decided to make a stop at the local Dairy Queen. Seeing as we did not have any money, we elected to stand in the drive-thru and drool over the glowing signs. It was the most beautiful thing I had ever seen. The way the ice cream looked, so perfect from the cone to the little swirly loop at the top, they almost looked like they were brought down from heaven by angels on little fluffy clouds.

As we looked at the detailed pictures of the ice cream cones and other frozen desserts, the manager of the store got on the intercom and asked us what we were doing in the drive-thru. We explained to him that we wanted some of these heavenly treats, but did not have any money. The manager suggested that we could pick up the miscellaneous change that people had dropped in the driveway, and if we got enough change, he would in return give us an ice cream cone.

At this point we would have been alright with manual labor, we had our minds set and we were not going to let this opportunity slip out of our hands. Jenny and I scurried around and picked up pennies and nickels off the black asphalt. We approached the manager with grins on our faces and our hands full of change, dirt and gravel. Our hard work got us two of those cones from heaven and still to this day I wonder if I am ever in need, will Dairy Queen let me clear their drive-thru of loose change in exchange for a frozen delight from heaven?

This "hokey" game was beginning to be a pretty remarkable way to break out of the daily routine of life, but little did I know that our fellow classmates had already seen us on the playground and when we did not come into class, it was reported to our principal. You can imagine how this is going to play out. I never knew that my love for leftover pizza would get me into trouble.

We arrived to Jenny's house and before we had time to start our afternoon of games and television, the phone rang. Rule number one; do not answer the phone when playing hokey. I don't think we read the instructions thoroughly because Jenny picked up the phone and on the other end was our school principal. We were directed to come back to school. I knew I was in trouble, but I did not know that my parents and the police had been called. You can imagine how upset my family was, but it did not compare to how angry my rump was after getting a swat that night.

That evening my mom was giving me my nightly bath. As she washed my hair, I was still crying from the day's event. I said to my mom with tears in my eyes, "She just asked me if I wanted to play a game called 'hokey'." It was then when she realized that the game I was describing was hooky and my mom later told me that she then thought to herself, "Maybe I was a little too hard on her."

The following years of school were pretty uneventful. I was a normal girl who liked the color pink, cabbage patch kid dolls, and stuffed animals. I loved being active and participated in gymnastics, dance, and began to learn how to play the flute. I began to recognize that when I put my mind to something, I found a way to make it happen. Just like when I was 10 years old and saw a Guinea pig in a pet store. I begged my Mom to buy it for me, but she stood firm with the idea that if I wanted that adorable rodent, I would have to work extra hard and save my allowance. My mom was trying to show me how hard it is to get money and save it.

Standing at 4 feet and 11 inches she was a ball of energy and her cheerfulness was infectious. She was patient with me when I came to her with absurd ideas.

Thinking of the weeks it would take to save my allowance, I knew that my guinea pig would be gone. I was not going to wait! I was the kind of girl that wanted everything yesterday and just felt I had to come up with the right plan. The moment we got home, I jumped out of the car and ran to the kitchen. My mom said, "What are you doing?" As I dug through our cabinets I said, "I am going to have a lemonade stand to raise the money for my guinea pig." My mom responded, "Alright, maybe you would like some help out to the corner." I grabbed a piece of paper and wrote in big letters, "Lemonade for a quarter" with a large smiley face.

For the next couple of hours, I stood on the corner and screamed my lungs out. Car after car pulled over and handed me dollar bills until I ran out of lemonade. I came home and bounced into the kitchen. "Mom, I think I have enough," grinning as I dumped all the change and bills that I had collected. We carefully counted my profits and then with a wink, my Mom said "I think you have enough, let's go get your pig." I was proud of that moment. I had wanted something and I made it happen. That day I got "Sugar", my guinea pig and even had enough money to buy her first bag of food.

In the sixth grade, I was envious of my brother Todd's Nintendo. He was a couple years older than I was and I had always tried to hang out with him but he never let me play that damn Mario Brothers video game.....yes, I am still bitter. There was a fund-raiser that our school put on each year; selling candy bars. But that year they threw in a curve ball. Whoever sold the most chocolate, got a brand new Nintendo.

A light bulb went on in my head. If I could win that contest, I would get my own gaming system so I would never have to ask my bother for anything ever again. Enter determination. My mind was set and that afternoon I began hitting up all of our neighbors. I was focused and ready to sell.

Truthfully, I don't remember how I did it, it was a big chocolate blur, but I sold 256 candy bars. I may have threatened neighbors and family or maybe I ate them. No one knows the truth, but I had a good feeling that I had won the contest. During homeroom announcements, the results were read. My principal congratulated everyone that participated, blah, blah, blah. His words were annoying and seemed to go on forever, like he was trying to bother me on purpose. Then he said, "And the student who sold the most candy bars wins the grand prize today.... and the winner is.....Allison Smith." I won the contest, I won the Nintendo! No more would I have to beg my brother to play, and he probably would think I was a pretty cool sister...ah, a bonus! This was the first time I knew that I could accomplish anything that I put my mind to.

Chapter 2:
Lucky Number 13

I was so proud to wear my cheerleading uniform; I think I even slept in it!

My freshman year of High School was a thrilling year. I used my new found determination and decided that I wanted to get on the cheerleading squad. I would spend hours practicing; before school, at lunch break, after school, and before I went to bed. We lived in a beautiful home in Pueblo West, Colorado where I had huge pink bedroom complete with a white lacquer waterbed. I would invite some friends over after school so we could practice our cheerleading skills. I knew I was not as good as all of the other girls trying out for the squad, but I had passion. That drive got me onto the cheerleading squad and the first day of High School, I got to wear my uniform with pride. My life couldn't get much better.

My brother, Todd, and I lived in the basement of our home, while my parents lived upstairs. It was perfect to have friends over because we felt alone and independent. You would think that my brother and I would just sit around and play video games together, but we had much more fun trying to get on each other's nerves. Todd would love to come into the living room and just change the television when I was watching it. He loved to tell my friends or boys who I thought were cute, that I picked my nose, or that I still sucked my thumb and slept with my baby blanket, which was kind of true.... As a 13 year old girl, this was heavy retaliation.

I would like to tell you that I was a perfect angel, but I would be lying. I spend multiple hours scheming on how to get my revenge. Then I had my chance. Todd had a pair of *Oakley* sunglasses which he would treat like they were gold; they would never leave his side. But on rare occasions, he left them next to the sink in the bathroom we shared. Thinking of all the times he had made fun of me or hurt my feelings, I worked up the courage to hit him where it hurts. I picked up those beautiful black glasses with the mirrored lenses and I put a scratch right down the middle of them with the metal plug of my blow-dryer. "That will teach him," I thought to myself. The only lesson learned that day was to deny any fault to the Oakley mutilation and that sibling rivalry did not define our relationship, it went deeper than that.

It was in my freshman year of high school that I had an epiphany. My life was not going the way I had planned. My brother and I fought constantly. As much as I loved being a cheerleader, the girls on the squad were evil. But worst of all, I began to notice my body was changing. Things that I could do with ease became a chore. I lost a lot of weight and my skin color began to have a greyish hue. It became hard to open a door or even hold a pencil, and if that wasn't enough, the girls on the squad starting treating me like I had a contagious disease. I thought that I was an important part of the team and that the squad would take care of its own, but I was ostracized for my differences. I spent many games and practices sitting on the bench. I would get such bad joint flare-ups that they prevented me from functioning, but the next day, I would be back to normal. I would lie and say that I twisted my ankle, so people would not know that I was hiding my declining health.

I was diagnosed with Juvenile Rheumatoid Arthritis (JRA) when I was 13 years old, my freshman year of high school. Every 2 to 4 weeks, my mom would pick me up from school and drive me to the medical center where Doctors would scratch their heads and try to make sense of the peculiar diagnosis. Every 4 weeks, I would have to come in for my monthly blood draw, just to ensure that my medications were not affecting my vital organs.

My mom had taken me out of my last class of the day to partake in our monthly medical nightmare. If it was challenging enough to be teenager but I was doing it with a degenerative, chronic illness and being pulled out of school only added to my feelings of being different. That day I was scheduled for my standard blood draw, the only problem was I was terrified of needles. As I was doing my normal tantrum, trying to squeeze some sympathy out of my mom, a gorgeous man came into the room.

As he scuttled across the floor towards me with a smile on his face, the mystery man said "Hello Allison, I am going to be doing your blood draw today," as he began opening drawers and gathering medical supplies. I could not respond; he looked like Kirk Cameron from my favorite show Growing Pains. I had spent many days coating my walls with his posters and reading every Tiger Beat Magazine so I could fantasize what it would be like to meet him in person. Here was my moment. Kirk had come to my small town of Pueblo, Colorado just to take my blood sample. And there was no way in hell I was going to look like an idiot! I pulled myself together and tried to act like getting a needle shoved into my arm was not a big deal.

The look-alike excused himself to go find some missing supplies he needed. The moment his dreamy smile disappeared into the other room, I shrieked "Did you see him mom? He is so cute!" My mom just snickered and said, "So now you are not afraid of needles?" Before I could respond, Kirk's twin reappeared. I sat up straight and glared at my mom, hoping she would control herself. He sat down on a stool and pushed the chair in my direction with such ease, he almost appeared to float towards me.

I placed my arm on the table next to me as he tied it with a plastic tourniquet. I began to get nervous about the pending needle, but I dare not show any fear. He wiped my arm with an alcohol swab, and my mom blurted out "Allison was afraid to get her blood drawn until she saw that you were so cute." I turned red with embarrassment as I barked out, "Mom!" I was mortified, but it was a small moment in my teenage life where I could forget that I had an auto immune disease and just be a normal girl. Nevertheless, I still have not forgiven her for ruining my chances with Kirk that day.

My parents had decided that due to my father needing work, we would have to move to Arizona, where he had a job waiting for him. My brother was two years older, so he had already moved to Tempe to attend Arizona State University. Since this happened at the beginning of my senior year, my parents decided that they would live in different states while I finished my last year of high school. I was ecstatic to know I would not have to leave my friends at County High in Pueblo, Colorado. Even though the school was surrounded by corn fields and was a 40 minute drive from home, I had a decent amount of friends and had become comfortable with maintaining my health with JRA. That was until a higher power started to make me feel guilty.

A few houses down from us lived a pastor of a community church and his wife. When his wife heard about my family living apart for my last year, she took it upon herself to have a spiritual talk...with me. She had this beautiful patio that was made out of a light color cedar wood and had a decent view of Pueblo Reservoir. She always wore too much makeup and appeared to have put it on in the dark, so her eyeliner was not at her eyelash line, but looked more like the eye black that football players use to reduce the glare of the sun. I don't think that she needed to worry about being tackled, seeing as she masked her scent with perfume that smelled like turpentine and kept small animals away. I was grateful we would be on her outdoor patio.

The pastor's wife had asked me to stop by after school so we could chat. I would have rather put a hot poker through my eye, but she was nice and always had cookies. After being let in, she directed me to carry two glasses of iced tea out to the patio. I walked slowly over her white shag carpet, being sure not to spill a drop of tea. As I got to the patio door, I noticed that she had already set out some cookies on a plate conveniently placed in between two wooden chairs. I could hear her whistling a song from the kitchen as I set the two drinks on the end table and removed my backpack. I took a seat, pretending to be observing how beautiful the reservoir looked, but truthfully, I was going over the details of my covert operation to steal a cookie.

I could hear her whistling getting louder, and the scent of her perfume got stronger as she appearing in the doorway. She took a seat next to me and let out a long sigh as she reached for her glass of iced tea. "I heard that your Daddy got a job offer in Arizona, what great news!" she chimed. "Yeah, I guess so." I responded while looking down at my backpack. "I also heard that you and your mom might be staying here alone in that big house of yours, just so you can finish your senior year, is that correct?" She inquired. "Yep, I don't want to leave my friends," I answered. "Now, you understand that a husband and wife need to be together in order to properly care for their family," she said as she nodded, "Don't you?"

Now I was starting to get irritated, I thought, "Why is she talking to me like I am a little kid, I understand how a family works." I couldn't care less about the mission to steal cookies, I just wanted to leave. I looked down and started to pick at my fingernails. She continued, "I am only telling you this because you and your mom staying behind and not having your Daddy around would cause a lot of tension in their marriage. You don't want to be the reason they get divorced, do you?" I felt like someone had punched me in the stomach. The thought that my selfishness could lead to the demise of my family made me sick. That evening, I told my mom that I wanted to move to Arizona so our family could be together. I never told her what brought on my sudden change of thought. We made the move the summer before my senior year.

Chapter 3:
The best years of my life?

Senior Pics, after moving to Arizona. I am the one on the right...

They say that the best years in your life are when you are a young adult. Whoever "they" are should be fired from their job. "They" should focus on not being an expert on everything, but maybe find another occupation. I found my way through my senior year at a new school in Arizona. It almost felt as if I had moved to a new state to start college early. I enrolled in beauty school to become a licensed manicurist. My father did not like the delay in attending college, but I enjoyed meeting people and hearing their stories. You would be shocked at what people tell their manicurist or hairdresser! I started dating a man named Jake, who was sweet and treated me like I was the most important thing in the world. I was beginning to start to feel somewhat like a normal person, until one day I found blood in my stool.

Just like many people who have problems with their digestive system, I tried to blame my issues on other factors. Maybe I ate something bad, or I was stressed, but it started to get worse and painful. During this confusion, Jake and I were getting closer, and I felt what it was like to be in love. He was romantic and always made a point to surprise me with little gestures of his heart. One night we were walking my parent's yellow lab down to the local park. Little did I know at the time, he had gone to the park earlier and placed a rose by the tree we liked to sit under; then he came to my house and asked me to go for a walk. He took me to that park and asked me to marry him that night. There was nothing else in the world that I wanted more.

We had a beautiful wedding on Valentine's Day in 1998 at our family Methodist church and then the reception in my parent's backyard. They both had this incredible eye for landscaping and a passion for gardening, so their backyard was the perfect choice. We moved to Tucson together and began our lives in a new city. It was just us against the world. I began to feel somewhat normal, but I was still having bowel issues. My physician diagnosed me with Ulcerative Colitis and I began trying various medications to control the bleeding, bloating, and pain.

When I was not responding to any medication other than Prednisone (a steroid that works great but has horrible side effects), my family doctor sent me to a gastroenterologist for further testing. I had the opportunity to spend the day at the hospital doing various tests. First they start with a manual exam. I like to call this the "getting to know you" exam. The facility I went to must like to get to know a lot of their patients, because they had their own special chair. You kneel on a soft leather seat, kind of like you are in a pew praying to God. Which I found ironic, seeing as how in a minute the doctor might just put you in that mood. I was wearing that exquisite hospital gown, you know the one that ties in the back; it is so freeing! Kneeling, I was directed to lie across, face down, on a flat surface. At that moment, I actually found it kind of comfortable, until the chair takes off like a rocket, launching me ass first up in the air until I was eye to eye (poor choice of words) with the doctor.

When I found myself in this position, along with an intern staring at my cash and prizes, I thought to myself, "This has got to be one of those caught on camera television shows, and any moment now, the host of the show is going to barge in with a microphone to catch my reaction. I just hope he knows which end is up." Feeling very awkward, the only thing I could come up with was, "So.....How about those Broncos?"

After being violated by a misleading chair, I was sent on to do an x-ray with Barium. I was handed a cup with a drink that is thick like a milkshake, but tastes like concrete. Then I rolled around in various positions on the x-ray table as they took pictures. With as much dining on concrete milkshakes and manual exams I endured, you would think I was on a hot date.

When that did not work, they decided to do a colonoscopy. If you have not had the honor of being invited to this party, you can live vicariously through me. The day before, I was directed to only drink clear liquids. Then I had to chug enough laxatives that could have made a moose cry. Then I saddled up to ride that porcelain pony until the sunset. This will ensure that the Doctors will be able to get a clear picture to properly diagnose any health issues. Giddy up!

The next day, I was placed under something called *Twilight*; no, this did not mean I was forced to watch endless hours of a love story between a vampire and a girl. It was considered to be a "conscious sedation" whatever the hell that means, seeing as there is nothing conscious about it. After I was wheeled into the procedure room, I could see four nurses scampering around the doctor. Then the machine that would be violating me while of course filming the whole thing, came into my line of vision. It consisted of a long black tube with a camera and a light on the end of the probe. I do not know why it is so long, it is not like we are circling the globe with it!

The doctor in his calmest voice said, "Alright, now take a nice deep, breath and try to relax." I thought to myself, "I want to cause him physical pain! Relax? Let's reverse the roles Doc, and you get on the table." Once on my side, the nurse said, "O.K. start counting from 100 backwards." I nodded in agreement and then I went under. Something that you might begin to see is that nothing is ever easy for me. If there is a possibility of something going wrong, I will take that adventure. Just like my colonoscopy. It appears that everything went well, when in fact I woke up in the middle of the procedure. Talk about a nightmare! The nurse was able to sedate me and then I woke up calmly hours later.

After my results came back from the colonoscopy, it was determined that I had pre-cancerous polyps and a more aggressive form of treatment needed to be explored. I tried to stay positive and keep on track with my life goals. Jake and I had bought our first home in Tucson. I really embraced the home life atmosphere and enjoyed decorating my new house. I continued to work as a manicurist, and Jake stayed busy in the medical field.

Jake worked as a Paramedic and was stationed out of a fire station in Tucson. This meant that he would work 24 hour shifts. It was hard to be alone some nights. One evening, I woke up to the glow of the television coming from the living room. In my middle of the night haze, I tried to logically explain how this could be happening, seeing as Jake was at work. I sat up in my bed and squinted, hoping to create a logical explanation. I rolled over onto my stomach and peered over the edge of the bed and saw that my dogs were laying on their beds on the floor. My basset hound Doc, started to yawn and slowly began to rise off the foam pet bed to make his way to the living room.

"There had to be a logical reason as to why the television was on...maybe Jake had a traumatic call and they released him from work to come home early," I thought to myself. Just when I started to believe my hypothesis, I heard the television volume going up, and my hound began barking. I grabbed my cordless phone and jumped out of bed. I could feel the cold plastic of the phone in my hand as I gripped it with so much pressure I was afraid I might break it. I ran into my bathroom, shut and locked the door. I could hear my heartbeat as I tried to clear my head so I could create a logical plan. I looked down at the phone and pressed the numbers 9-1-1.

Pushing the receiver to my ear, I heard a woman's voice say, "911, what is your emergency?" I struggled to sound calm as I whispered "I think there is someone in my house...I am going to go check, but I wanted you on the phone just in case I need help." She responded, "Do not leave the bathroom...do you have a gun in the house? Try to get in the back of your closet and remain calm...help is on the way." Don't you love it when someone tells you "Just remain calm?" It is like they are asking me to throw sharp objects in their general direction.

I caught a glimpse of the current state of my appearance in the bathroom mirror. I was wearing a *Winnie the Pooh* getup, complete with a tank top and what the fashion designers call "boy-shorts", which is a politically correct way of saying "butt cheeks hanging out" undergarment. Then I had this logical thought that if I had to run from the person watching cable in my living room, I would need shoes. I glance down and grabbed the first pair of shoes that I saw; which were my black, strappy heels. Now, to complete my look, the night before I had not washed off my makeup. I was being lazy, so I just splashed water on my face and could care less if my mascara was running. I didn't blame my makeup...I would be running too!

I was fashionably ready for my cat walk out of the house. I could hear banging on my doors and windows, in my house, then a minute later came the helicopter, lights shining into my home. I was advised by the 911 operator that the police had arrived and to make my way to an exit. I thought the best plan of action was to run out of the closet into the garage and down my drive way to safety. I took a deep breath, unlocked the bathroom door and ran. I made it to the garage and threw the door open. An officer was standing in my garage and shining his flashlight in my face. He grabbed my wrist and pulled me to the side of his patrol car as six armed officers went running into my house. I was shivering from the excitement, or maybe it was due to my choice of clothing.

A couple of minutes passed as each room was checked for the stranger watching HBO on my couch. The officer next to me said, "Just a couple more minutes to make sure that it's safe." I waited patiently. A few minutes later, we hear a voice over the radio say, "It's clear, you can bring her in." As we enter the house, every cabinet, closet, and room was open with all the lights on. The police were holstering their guns as I walked into the living room. A tall, dark haired officer held up my television remote control and said, "I think we found the problem." Confused I leaned in to get a good look. The plastic had been chewed up. Which lead to my next question, "Why would the stranger watching HBO try to eat my remote?"

Yes, I am capable of having blonde moments, I give myself that right but this one was record breaking. I was a hot mess. Trying to remain patient the officer said, "Your dogs must have gnawed on it and accidently turned it on." As logical as that may sound, it did not add up in my head. I said, "But they were lying next to me when I woke up, they couldn't have done that." A few of the cops began to chuckle. The officer said "Maybe they chewed up the remote, turned on the television and then came back to bed." He was nodding his head when the light bulb came on in mine. I thought to myself, "Oh my...I am dumb." At that moment, I came back to reality just enough to notice what I was wearing. I looked down at my magnificent strappy heels that accentuated my booty shorts and *Winnie the Pooh* attire. I jumped over the couch, grabbed a pillow and covered myself. As I was walking slowly backwards I said, "We don't need to file a report, right?" The officer grinned and said, "No, we're alright, have a good night."

Standing in my kitchen with every cabinet open, Doc comes in and I swear that dog's face was saying "You are an idiot.....now give me a treat!" I looked down at him, shook my head and mumbled, "We won't tell Jake about this." I turned off the lights and began to walk to the bedroom with my strappy heels clicking on the floor. The next morning, I was getting the newspaper in my drive way. I can see my neighbor in his bathrobe, drinking his cup of coffee. I smile and wave. He lifts his coffee up and says, "How's your remote control?" Turns out, he worked for the police and got the story from the other officers about my eventful evening. I thought to myself, "Guess I better tell Jake....."

Chapter 4:
In the Beginning

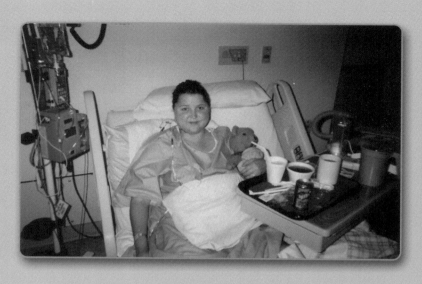

Yes, that is me...I did explain that I was very sick.
This is in November 2001, my first colon surgery.

*T*here are moments in one's life when the reality which they created, will never be the same. Within a minute of our existence, there is a shift where we become inconveniently conscious. Life is full of these markers, and it is not the marker itself that is significant, but our reaction the change. On November 1st 2001, my life changed forever. On that day, I had my first surgery for Colon Cancer, and it was that moment when I realized that my life, as I knew it, would never be the same.

Since I was young, my Physicians felt that my illness would be no threat, just an inconvenience. But after I endured 2 years of pain, passing blood, and gaining over 50 pounds from high doses of steroids, we knew something had to change. Baffled Doctors, with no alternative explanations, decided to send me to the professionals at Norris Cancer Center at University of Southern California (USC) in Los Angeles. It was decided that I would have a small portion of my colon removed. Who would have known all the amazing information you learn about your digestive system when you are ill? I have some mind-blowing random factoids that I reserve for special moments, like at a party, when I feel an awkward moment coming on; I can spout out all of the body parts that are involved in the process of a bowel movement.

The night before my surgery, Jake and I had made the long drive from Arizona to California. The first stop we made was at the Olive Garden to have my last dinner with my brother Todd and his now wife Beth before surgery. The concept of unlimited salad and breadsticks was not overlooked that evening. I ate like I was preparing to hibernate for the winter. Todd and Beth were asking me questions about the upcoming day; I just kept nodding my head, trying to make it appear as if I was listening, but focusing on anything was challenging. Beth has the awesome ability to make you feel like you are the most important person in the room. The way she focused on the conversation and was always curious about what was happening in my life. Todd is so fortunate to be married to her, and I am blessed that she is my sister-in-law.

I could not drown the voices in my head. "What the hell is happening to me? Why me? What did I do to deserve this?" I believe that if you treat people with respect and if you live a good life, you will be loved and cared for in return. I looked around the restaurant at the people eating and completely oblivious to my pain. I was alone. It did not matter that I had family to encourage me; I was the only one that was going to have their stomach cut open. How would they ever understand what I was going through? I felt like I was in the middle of the crowded restaurant screaming at the top of my lungs, and no one looked up.

As I said my good-byes to my brother, he said, "Are you going to keep your large intestine to wear as a necklace?" The thought of wearing my bowels around my neck was disgusting but hilarious. I burst into tears and laughter. Although my brother and I were never on good terms as children, I knew this was his way of letting me know he felt my pain and fear. He said, "Good luck tomorrow" and opened his arms. It is sad that it takes a horrible situation to make people recognize what is important in life. That evening, in front of my car, I hugged my brother for the first time.

I had to be at the USC Cancer Center early the following morning, so Jake and I decided to get a hotel room close to the hospital. In our room the queen size bed was centered in the middle of the room with a mattress that was so firm, it felt like I was lying on a piece of wood. After hours of tossing and turning I sat up in the dark room; I couldn't get comfortable in the stiff, bleached white sheets. In a cotton tank top, and underwear, I stood up and ran my fingers down towards my stomach. This would be the last time my tummy would be normal, I pushed that thought from my head knowing it would only lead to misery.

I looked around the room, squinting to identify any objects that were familiar. I could vaguely make out the outline of the television and dresser. I found my way to the window and pulled back the shades. The gleaming street lights invaded the hotel room and burned my eyes. As I sat down on the windowsill, the cold wood beneath me made my body shiver. When I leaned forward to peer through the window, my breath fogged the glass. Looking from the fourth floor I could see a row of taxi cabs which lined the curb below, and people standing on the sidewalk that appeared to only be black dots. They looked so small, almost like bugs scurrying around aimlessly.

It was in that moment that I felt insignificant, regardless of the journey I was about to embark on, my life seemed irrelevant. Looking at the people below, I felt sadness. We are all wrapped up in our daily schedules and personal drama, but ultimately we are alone; little ants scurrying around, bumping into each other but never connecting. Our time on earth seemed meaningless and empty.

The next day was a fog of paperwork and meeting people whose names I do not remember. My mom and dad were making the trip that day from Mesa, Arizona to be with me during the surgery, but traffic was slowing them down, and we were unsure if they would make it to the hospital before I went under anesthesia. The last thing I remember was seeing my parents run through a door. I felt calm as we said our good-byes. My mom began to break down, so my dad gently pushed her out of my line of vision as he continued to encourage me.

I woke up that evening unable to move or speak, but I could hear that my parents were in the room with me. I heard my dad say, "Go talk to your daughter." Then my mom responded, "She can't hear me." I slowly raised my hand and attempted to use sign language that my mom had taught me as a little girl. I made a fist, squeezing my fingers with all my strength. My mom was trying to interpret my words, "That's an "a"... no, it's the letter "s"....I don't know Ally," she said with frustration. I tried again, "s-i-c-k". I was feeling nauseous and my mom began to understand what I was signing. She was ecstatic to finally be able to talk to her daughter again, and I was happy just to be alive.

My family surrounded my hospital bed and through bouts of tears they told me that the surgery was much more challenging than had been anticipated. The doctors had removed my full large intestine, rectum, and part of my small intestine due to infection. They had created an internal pouch that would act as my colon and with luck, I would be able to get back to a normal life. But in the meantime, the surgeon had made a small incision in my pelvic area and pulled my intestine through that hole. A plastic bag covered this incision. This is what I most feared, I had a colostomy bag.

The following days after my surgery, I did not want to leave the comfort of my narcotic haze or my bed. I was only allowed "chips and sips" which in medical lingo, meant chips of ice and sips of water, a typical diet after abdominal surgery. I grabbed the television remote and tried to clear my head with mindless channel surfing. I found it ironic that when my diet was restricted to chips of ice, the most detailed and delicious food commercials appear to dominate the screen. I am not sure who does the photography for these restaurants, but they are amazing. They could make halibut-mustard-custard look appetizing.

While watching the morning news, the camera panned to an attractive anchorwoman who began to talk about a recent bank robbery in Los Angeles. She smiled at the camera in her beige pant suit and finished hair. I began to feel a rush of anger. I resented the fact that this woman had been able to get up with her picture-perfect family, eat her delightful breakfast, shower, and slap on her flawless makeup. Then she drove to her perfect job, in her astounding car and smiled at the world on camera, showing how great her life was. But I was stuck in a hospital bed going through my personal hell. I despised her for that.

On the third day, I progressed to clear liquids. The taste of jello and apple juice was divine. The stink from my lack of showering wafted into the hallway towards the nurse's station. My mom had been trying to get me up to shower, but I did not want to do anything. The pain emotionally and physically was excruciating. That morning a plump nurse wearing purple scrubs with green elephants that paraded across her chest came whistling into my room, walked directly to the window and opened the blinds. Her cheerfulness was nauseating.

I usually found comfort in the sun, but now it annoyed me and for a second, I thought of throwing my jello at her head. She came over to the side of my bed and in the sweetest voice said, "Time to get up and make your bed. I am going to help you to the chair and then we can get you cleaned up! It will make you feel better!" With her assistance, I changed into a new gown and dowsed my body with a fruity spray, hoping that it would cover up the fact that I had not showered in days. Although my bitterness towards the world did not allow me to admit it, the nurse was right, I did feel better.

By the end of the week, I could not stay in the hospital anymore. The smell of the stale air was revolting. Armed with my trusty I.V. pole, my parents loaded me up in a wheelchair and we made our way to the sliding doors of the entrance. Although I still had a catheter in my arm and no understanding of how to care for my new colostomy appliance, I had to fight the urge to run away from that building.

Outside of the Hospital, there was a beautiful courtyard complete with rose gardens and a small food cart. As we exited the building, a light breeze of fresh air came over my body. The sun warmed my skin and the wheelchair that carried me felt like freedom. We found shade under a large tree. There were people strolling around in the courtyard; they all seemed to be late for something important, but I was standing, or shall we say sitting still?

My parents made superficial conversation such as what my brother's new apartment looked like and how bad the traffic was in California. As I was staring at the concrete below me, a little black bird bounced up to where we were sitting. He kept his space, but was interested in our presence. I would like to think that my new friend's interest was strictly about treats that we might have for him, but his curiosity was most likely due to the smell of fruity spray and three days of not bathing that I was releasing.

As he got the nerve, he would hop a little closer as he cocked his head at us. Then two more black birds arrived. They tested each other's bravery as they bounced around my feet. I began to laugh and although it hurt like hell, I felt a ton of bricks was being lifting off my chest. I said to my parents, "We should name him," as I pointed to the first bird that had come to visit. My mom responded, "What would you call him?" and I have no reason why, most likely the drugs were talking, but I blurted out, "Flea!" My mom looked at me with a confused look and said, "Umm....alright. Flea it is."

My concerned mom felt that I needed to go back to the room, just in case the nurses needed me or the Doctor came to visit. I asked if we could go see the flowers before we went up. I wanted to see something other than saline, plastic, and metal which had been my world for the last few days. My dad rolled me over to the roses and Flea followed us. I leaned forward and pressed my nose into a pink rose; the soft petals tickled. I took a deep breath, and the fragrance overwhelmed my senses. For that one moment, I felt alive again.

Two weeks slowly drifted by until it was decided that I could fly back to Tucson. I had gotten to the point that I could not tolerate being in my hospital room again. I would walk the halls, travel to the courtyard, watch the fish in the tank in the admissions area, and every time I went outside, Flea was waiting for me. Since the Physicians couldn't tie me to the bed, I was able to prepare to go home. I was directed to wait twelve weeks for my body to have a chance to heal, and then I could come back to the Norris Cancer Center to have my colostomy bag reversed. I flew home with my mom that afternoon.

As I was healing at home, everything was more challenging, but it was nice to have my family around to cook and clean for me. Adjusting to the colostomy bag was a whole new battle. I decided that if I were to accept this situation, my bag and I would have to get a little better acquainted, it needed a name. The term *Stoma* referred to the part of my intestine that protruded out of my body. II named it "Steve the Stoma", which almost sounds like a cartoon superhero.

Adapting to having an appliance collect your stool instead of, shall we say, "going number 2" was difficult. The mechanics of it alone was creepy. I had to be careful to not let stool rest against my skin for too long, or it would start to break down my flesh. Not only was it painful, but the products that you use to help the bag create a seal, stung like bitch, and I am not referring to a female dog, as you can imagine. But just like everything in my life, it was complicated. The colostomy bag would not hold a seal to my skin, and almost daily my bag would leak or break, which is not very appealing if you were around other people. I had to carry an extra colostomy bag with me everywhere. It was emotionally draining to be thinking about that potential every day, but I tried to stay positive and keep in mind that this was all temporary. Just like my favorite quote, "This too shall pass," and it did.

I made the journey back to California twelve weeks after my initial surgery to reverse my colostomy bag. This means that they would reconnect my intestine and my friend "Steve the Stoma" would be gone. Then I would be able to use my internal pouch. Just to clarify, my pouch is not a place to store loose change or candy; it would act as a storage area for my stool. The only drawback is that my pouch would be much smaller than my large intestine, so I would have to use the restroom 5-10 times a day. I did not care, I was just happy to be free from the nightmare of having a colostomy bag.

I went in for the second surgery and a few hours later, came out feeling great. I went home and got ready to tackle the world. I wanted to make up for lost time, but there was one little problem, I had a small leak in my abdominal cavity that was unknown for months. Within those months I was in and out of the hospital as Doctors tried to figure out why I was running a fever and vomiting. I left my local Doctors scratching their heads, so it was decided that I would have to go back to California to have the specialist take a look at me.

My husband and I got into the car and began heading for the coast. We stopped at a hotel in Placentia, California and decided to go to bed early. I woke up in a dark hotel room around three o'clock in the morning. I was running a fever, vomiting, and was confused as to why we were in California. Jake called

911, and I was rushed to a nearby hospital. I was going in and out of consciousness and hallucinating, to be truthful, I do not really remember this evening. I was going Septic and my body was shutting down. They found a fistula in my abdominal area, which was leaking infection into my abdominal cavity and in my weak state, I was dying.

I was fortunate that where I was in California was not far from The Norris Cancer Center. An ambulance drove over an hour to get me to the Doctors that could help. I was being wheeled into the hospital on a gurney, hooked up to an I.V. and Oxygen. I was quietly singing to myself "Let it Be" by the Beatles. I was not really in my body at this moment. I know this might sound ludicrous, but it was like I was watching myself from a distance. I could hear the Paramedic reporting to the nurse about my current state, but the words were unrecognizable. I looked to my right where a tree and some shrubbery covered a picnic table; probably for the nurses taking a coffee break. Then, emerging from the plants was my familiar little black bird, Flea. It was like my friend knew I was coming back. I must have said his name out loud, because the nurse walked over to me and said in the most childish voice, "You see the birdy?" I stared at her, confused as to why she was treating me like I was mentally challenged. I did not respond.

I was wheeled towards the emergency room entrance, as the medical staff kept talking about me like I was not there. We reached the automatic doors to the hospital and as they opened a breeze of air brushed over my face, and I started to cry. The smell of the hospital brought all the painful memories back into my body. I will, by no means, forget that smell, and I pray to God that I never have to go back to that hospital.

I had a laparoscopic procedure that was to be less invasive, but the pain was just as excruciating as my past abdominal surgery. It was almost Easter, and I did not care about chocolate bunnies or jelly beans, I just wanted to go home. My visit was not anticipated so my parents had not prepared to take time off from work, but that did not stop my Dad. Before I was out of the operating room the first day, he was on his way with his Ford Bronco, (which is a requirement of a true Coloradan, along with a yellow lab and hiking boots) equipped with a mattress in the back, so I could get home in comfort. It was my very own Daddy ambulance and I was getting the V.I.P treatment!

I had always loved my Dad; we had a special connection. He was so patient and calm with me, and although he appeared collected when I saw him, I knew that car ride all alone to California was torture. He had no clue of what condition his only daughter was in and he had no idea how to help me.

This is the point in my life where things begin to get blurry. I like to believe that your body has a way of protecting itself when you sustain trauma. I forgot in what order things happened or the exact details of the next two years, but I was in a bad place. Every possible complication that could happen found its way into my life. I sustained a blood clot, kidney stones, an abscess, another fistula, bowel obstructions, and multiple infections. This required many procedures and countless nights in the hospital. I had become a professional patient. I could even tell the doctors what I.V. cocktail of medications I needed when I came through the emergency room. I even had a pre-packed bag for any medical emergency that might arise, and I knew each item that was necessary to bring with me to make the hospital a little tolerable.

Something that I had noticed up to this point was that being the patient means that you receive flowers and get-well cards. You have family and friends visiting and sharing stories about happy or silly memories, but the spouse is somehow forgotten. Jake never got flowers, or cards. He was left with dealing with the potential of losing his wife while trying to provide for us, run the house, and all while caring for me. All of his needs and wants for his life were swept away with the wind. It had become all about me, not by choice but by necessity. You begin to take on these pseudo roles of patient and caregiver, not husband and wife. This was very hard on us as a couple. If we could survive my declining health, could our marriage survive?

Chapter 5:
May 5th, 2003

Todd and I enjoying an afternoon together.

*T*hen my life came to a dead stop on May 5th, 2003. You know it's bad if you remember the exact date. Jake had left that morning for a 24 hour shift at the fire station and I was alone laying on the couch trying to rest. At the time, we had two basset hounds, Doc and Wyatt, who I loved like I had birthed them myself. Doc resembled "Jabba the Hut", except he was not green. Doc was, shall we say, fluffy. He was 90 lbs and his belly almost dragged on the floor. He was slow in agility and brains, but he knew how to drool like a pro. Wyatt on the other hand was smaller, smarter, and loved his mommy. I was resting on our denim blue couch, watching random movies. It was around lunch time and I was feeling miserable. My body was weak and I felt like I was running a fever.

Tucson was hot in May, but I was shivering so violently, Wyatt came to check on me. I petted the top of his head and said "Mommy doesn't ......" and before I could finish my sentence, I could feel the vomit coming up my throat. I gripped the side of the couch as another contraction clutched my stomach. My first thought was to call Jake. I was terrified, and I knew he would make me feel safe. Wyatt began to whimper. He was feeling helpless as I tried to sit up on the couch. I thought I had heard the television in the background as I strained to rise to my feet, but then I recognized the voice, it was me. I was repeating "Get to the phone, Get to the phone."

It was such a surreal moment, it felt like a dream. I rolled off the couch and crawled to the phone and with no hesitation, I called 911. I could hear the ambulance in the distance as I lay on my kitchen floor; Wyatt never left my side. When the paramedics arrived I was apologetic, I didn't mean to misuse the ambulance and the Paramedics on something that I did not feel was severe; I thought I just might have the flu. They helped me to my feet and placed me on a gurney. I was being rolled out of my house, when I glanced back. Wyatt was at the window watching me.

After the initial tests of x-rays and blood work, I was left in the emergency room alone. The glow of the hospital lights shined like a spotlight on my bed. The sheets were stiff, but the pain in my stomach was distracting. The nurse had given me I.V. pain medication, and I remember thinking how bizarre it was that I was still in pain, which had never happened before. Hours passed when a man came into my room and introduced himself as a Dr. Melcer, a surgeon. It seemed like I had floated out of my body, and I was watching myself from a corner in the room. Dr. Stuart Melcer informed me that I had ruptured open somewhere in my abdominal cavity and my tummy was filling with blood and stool. In a state of shock, I said "I have to get back to California... they have to save my internal pouch," and the doctor said, "No way. You will die".

He explained that if I had fallen back asleep at my house, I would have died; my body would have just stopped functioning. I could not process what he was saying any longer. I began to sob. I called 911 at 12 noon and by 4 pm I was on the operating table. This moment changed my life forever; I still have an eerie feeling on May 5th each year that passes. No margaritas or tacos for me; I just think about where my life has been and how shocking it is that I am still alive.

My parents lived in Mesa, and I was two hours south in Tucson, which did not give them enough time to see me before I went under. There were multiple unknowns going into this surgery; we were unsure if I was going to be able to keep my internal pouch, they also did not know what condition my body was in. I decided to make one more phone call to my mom before they began the procedure.

When my mom answered the phone I said, "Mom, I want to tell you something." I could hear in the background her frantic pace as she packed her belongings to come to the hospital had stopped. She responded, "Ok, what is it?" I felt hot tears flooding my eyes as I said, "If I die, I would like to be buried with my "Blue Blakin" and teddy." On the other end of the phone my mom did not respond, she began to weep. I did not have this conversation with her to upset her; I logically thought I was about to die. I knew that my body could not sustain itself much longer at the rate my illness was progressing.

I detailed what flowers I liked and how hard my death would be on Jake. But the one detail I could not make clear in my head was if I wanted to be cremated or buried. Neither option seemed appealing. A nurse came into my room to transport me to the pre-surgical room. I said one last time, "I love you mom," and then I hung up. I felt strangely calm knowing that I might never see my family again. I was still in shock; I expected to wake up from this nightmare in my bed, at home with my dogs.

There were no planned surgeries, seeing as it was a holiday. I was wheeled into a large room that had empty beds lined in a row against a wall. As I manipulated the tubes from my I.V. so I could changed into the surgical gown, I looked up and realized I was alone. The sound of my bare feet walking on the tile floor echoed throughout the room. The tile was cold and seemed to radiate through my body. I began to weep quietly until the sound of a person walking at a frantic pace pulled me out of my misery. Jake ran into the room and as we locked eyes, we both began to tear up. I could breathe again; the weight of my pain was temporarily removed. The last thing I remember is Jake hugging me.

I woke up ten days later in agony. My mother and Jake were at the side of my bed. There was a tube coming out of every orifice in my body. Dr. Melcer had lost I.V. access during surgery, which led to having a port placed in my chest; which is known as the Cadillac of I.V. access. I had a feeding tube down my nose, which made breathing strenuous. I pulled off the tubing that was providing me oxygen and I said, "Am I alright?" My mom went on to explain that I went septic again, and Dr. Melcer felt my body needed time to rest, so I was placed into a Morphine coma for almost a week. Confused and cloudy, I tried to sit up when I noticed a very familiar feeling. I touched my stomach and ran my hand down to my pelvic area where I felt plastic. My colostomy bag had somehow found its way onto my body again. I began to scream. My mom tried to calm me, but it was no use. The hell I knew had become reality once more.

I was taking a large amount of pain medication, so I was not all the way there if you know what I mean. I noticed that not only did the narcotics alleviate any physical pain, it eased emotional pain. So on the dot, every four hours, I would be hitting the nurse's button to request pain meds. It was a vicious cycle. I began to notice that even when I was drugged up and sleeping at night, my body would wake up every four hours. I was creating a physical addiction to the medications, and if it continued, I would have a new coping technique for the emotional pain.

I noticed that my Dad had been in and out of my room at the hospital. When I asked him about it, he responded, "I could have put a cardboard cutout of myself in the corner of your hospital room, and you would have thought I was there." We both laughed, it was true! My Dad had been staying at our home in Tucson feeling helpless and decided to build us a covered patio. He spent hours putting it together and building it. It was the only thing he could think of doing, investing his fear and frustration into a project that would create something beautiful.

When I was released from the hospital, I was put on suicide watch and was not to be left alone for any length of time. My cousin and uncle came into town to relieve my parents. We watched movies as I slept the days away. Everyone tried to encourage me and keep my spirits up, but I was giving up. Trying to fight for my existence was a battle I was losing. I could not eat food for weeks, which would allow my body to recover. I had to wear a backpack that was full of a milky white I.V. solution called total parenteral nutrition (TPN). This fluid contained all the nutrients that I needed to survive and it was pumped slowly into my body through the port in my chest. It was undecided if I could ever use my internal pouch again, and the thought of having a colostomy bag before I was 25 years old sickened me.

I wanted to die. I would have if I could have found a painless way to do it. The emotional sorrow and the physical agony had weakened my spirit. Jake came home from his shift to find me in the kitchen. I had a nurse that came to my home to teach me how to flush my port, so it wouldn't get infected. As the needle was pushed into my port in my chest, I screamed. I could not take one more ounce of pain. Everything hurt, especially my heart. I had so many wishes and hopes for my life. Cancer ripped my dreams right out of my body and left me in the darkness.

Every day was a struggle; I did not want to get out of bed. I welcomed sleep because my dreams were the only break I could get from my life. I had lost the fight in me. Jake could see it, so one afternoon he came to me and said, "If you can't fight for yourself, fight for me......for us." It was like my spirit just slapped me in the face. I knew I could get through this. I knew I was strong. I just needed someone to believe in me. To this day, I know with all my heart, that without Jake in my life, I would have given up.

I pushed myself to keep moving, and with the encouragement of my family each day got a little easier. I was getting stronger and finding things to occupy my time. My doctors had been encouraging me to quit school, file for disability, and focus on my health. But I refused to listen to them. I enrolled at The University of Arizona majoring in Psychology. Going back to school was surreal. I walked around campus like I was a normal girl trying to find her place in the world, but deep down inside, I knew how fragile life was. I lived in fear of the when the other shoe would drop and put me back in the hospital.

I kept the secret of my colostomy bag from everyone; I was afraid of how they would look at me. There was not one semester during my undergraduate studies that I wouldn't be in the hospital for complications. Kidney Stones, abscesses, or bowel obstructions, take your pick, I had them all; but I was determined to make up for lost time. I tried to embrace the moments when I was not in the hospital.

In my junior year at The University of Arizona, I had almost forgotten the pain of the last three years. Visiting Dr. Melcer, he said, "I have good news and bad news......which would you like to hear first?" I thought to myself for a moment and replied, "Bad news, let's get it out of the way." He looked down, sighed and said, "Due to the complications that you have endured, it is not recommended that you get pregnant. The weight of a baby on your internal pouch would be too much, and you have way too much scar tissue, in fact we are not even sure you can get pregnant." I just kept pushing forward; I did not want to process anymore emotional crap. I responded, "What is the good news?" Dr Melcer smiled and said, "I feel confident that we can try to reverse your colostomy bag. You have had over a year to heal, but if it continues to be a problem, we will have to go back to having a bag." It was like winning the lottery! After 14 months, I was able to go back into surgery and have the plastic parasite removed from my body.

I was determined to take care of myself, be healthy and get back to a normal life. I started Yoga at the University and began meeting some amazing friends. The stress of my illness had taken its toll on my marriage with Jake. We had both been cheated out of time in our young lives and found activities that did not include each other. I was devoted to school and fitness. I realized that if I stayed busy, I would not have to cope with my fear and anxiety that my poor health had brought on. The cancer had brought in an element that we couldn't face....our own mortality. After 6 years of marriage, Jake and I divorced and went our separate ways. I could not take care of our dogs alone anymore, so I found a home for them together with another family. The loss of my dogs was even more devastating because it meant I was now truly alone in this world.

Chapter 6:
Embracing the Madness

Only took a decade, but finally I graduated!

*I*f I were a cat, I would have blown through all of my nine lives and maybe a couple more. You cannot go through an experience like I had survived and not have a different thought process. I had this unbelievable urge to live every day to its fullest, to tell those I love how much they mean to me every day, and to find ways to help those who are facing the long battle of illness. After the dissolution of my marriage, I began to see there was no one to lean on. My parents lived hours away, so I became very independent and tried to believe that I did not need anyone, I could take care of myself.

I began to look at my health in a different light. I would take one surgery at a time, and if that was too much, I would take one day at a time, and if I couldn't do that, one minute at a time. I would slowly deal with a medical issue and then say, "O.K. what do we have to do next?" I used this method as I slowly worked through my undergraduate degree. Adjusting to a life that did not circle around my illness was sometimes difficult. Every day there were triggers that reminded me where I had been, and I knew it was not "if" I would be back in the hospital but "when".

I had gone to visit my parents for a long weekend vacation during the holidays. My sister-in-law Beth was pregnant and we had been planning a baby shower at a tea shop. The day was beautiful. Just being surrounded by family as my Mom and Dad were about to become grandparents was perfect. Mom and I had just gotten back to the house when I started feeling the very familiar abdominal pain. I tried to tell myself I was just overreacting and then the vomiting started. I had various medications that I could use when I need to stop vomiting, but none of them were working. My Dad said, "Why don't you go get some sleep? You have had a long day, maybe you are just tired." I smiled and said, "You are probably right...night Dad" and I slowly walked to the bedroom. I tried to rest, but the pain was excruciating.

Close to midnight, I was vomiting so violently the pain was bringing me to tears. I had lain down next to the toilet. The cold tile felt fantastic on my hot skin. I gripped the side of the toilet and hoisted myself off the floor. My bare feet dragged on the tile as I used all the strength I could muster to walk to my parents' bedroom door. My hands trailed against the wall as I passed the kitchen. The silence was deafening. I was alone in the dark. I felt the door and hit it with my palm; sound filled the room. My Mom flung open the door, almost like she had been standing there waiting for my knock. Her eyes squinted as she said, "Are you ok?" Through hot tears I replied, "No."

My parents got me into the car and over to the nearest hospital. I was placed in a wheelchair and rolled into the waiting area. I did not have the strength to hold my head up, let alone talk. The triage nurse took my vitals and said, "It's going to be awhile, we have a full house." I did not know how long I could wait, I could feel the vomit in the back of my throat and the pain was becoming unbearable. My mom was asking me questions, but all of her words just meshed together. My world was spiraling out of control. I began to gag, but the discomfort was unbearable. With all the strength I had left in my body, I said, "Help me........please, I can't do this," then I started vomiting. In between contractions, I kept repeating, "Help me.....please."

It pains me to think about the torment my health has brought onto my family. To watch your daughter's slow deterioration and know that there is not a single thing you can do to ease her suffering can only be shy of eternity in hell. My mom was lightly rubbing my back as she looked over at my father. No words needed to be said, my mom walked up to the nurse's desk and said, "She needs to see a Doctor now. She is too sick. Please help us."

Two men sat on chairs next to my father enjoying watching the drama of my affliction. I lift my head to see one of the men leaning over to the other one as he whispered, "Better lay off the booze next time, eh?" It did not take a second before my Dad confronted the men. Although I did not hear my Dad's response I can only imagine it had something to do with a shotgun or a baseball bat.

The evening involved my favorite tests, but I welcomed answers. I had a suspicion that it was bad when the nurse pushed my cocktail through my I.V. and the pain and vomiting did not stop. I was trying to focus on the television when I heard footsteps coming into my hospital room. The ER Doctor had appeared from behind the curtain with a serious face. I said, "What's wrong?" I felt like I wanted to run, but where could I go that my poor health wouldn't find me?

"It is your scan. You have a bowel obstruction. There is a loop of intestine that has toughened and is not allowing food to pass," the Doctor replied as he looked at the floor. I clenched the television remote with all my strength. I felt my face get flush as I tried to control my emotions. Whether I would scream or sob was unknown, so I just pushed it down. "What is the game plan?" I mumbled. Taking a deep breath, the Doctor replied, "NG tube is the first step, and then if that doesn't work, we might have to do surgery again." A nasogastric tube (NG) is put in your nose and down into your stomach. It is kind of ironic that reading the definition on paper does not do it justice.

I was asked by the nurse to sip water through a straw (which would allow me to swallow the tube), and then they held my head as they put the tube into my nose and slid it all the way until I could feel it in the back of my throat . I began to immediately gag and tried to push the nurses away. It took three attempts until they got it. This NG tube is like hell inside of hell. There are no words to describe it. When I tried to talk, I sounded like a 70 year old lounge singer who had smoked her whole life. If I moved, my gag reflex would cause me to vomit. If a nurse would try to adjust my NG tube, I would slap her hand. Hey, I never said I was a nice patient.

I spent the following days in the hospital in Mesa; my parents stayed with me during the day and tried to keep my spirits up. It was difficult to adjust to not having Jake there. At night when everyone went home, I was alone in the hospital. I can remember many nights of lying in my bed feeling terrified. The glow of the television was the only light on. I knew that if I were to push the button to call the nurse, she would promptly come in and check on me. But she was a stranger and I was ultimately alone. "Blue Blankin" became my comfort. I would have her in hand at all times. If it became too much, I would press her against my face and smell her. The smell reminded me of an innocent time as a child, when I was not ill. It brought a smidgen of comfort into my scary world.

The NG tube was successful in alleviating my bowel obstruction, and after almost a week in the hospital, I was released to go home. My body was angry but I was happy that I had averted a surgical procedure. I spent a couple more days at my parent's home and then began my slow journey back to Tucson.

My life was unpredictable. Each day brought a new adventure, and I never knew where it would take me. I would like to say that I began to embrace this madness that became my life. I had accepted that I would live my life with medical challenges. I was choosing not to let it define me. In fact, it would almost be difficult if my life was normal; I wouldn't know what to do with myself! I was still Allison, the cheerful and bubbly girl I had always been, but I had a unique gift of being an old soul. I had lived a lot of life in my short time on earth.

It was a hot sunny day in Mesa, Arizona. I had come up to visit my family for the weekend, and for once, I had no medical crap to partake in. We decided to go to the grocery store and pick up some food to make dinner.

My dad owned a white Ford Escape that oozed testosterone. It had a first aid kit, granola bars, loose change, tools, pop up chairs, and a roll of toilet paper in the glove box. It smelled like lumberjacks, body odor, and flannel. I was sitting in the back seat as we pulled into a parking spot.

My mom opened the door, and a wave of heat from the black asphalt rushed over my skin. I was maneuvering my body out of the back seat with as much focus as Houdini preforming a magical act. With my mom holding the door, I was unaware that my t-shirt had gotten snagged in the seat belt. As it rose up and exposed my belly, I heard my mom say, "Pull that down, no one wants to see that," as she tugged on my shirt. My world crashed at that very moment. I had been through so much that I felt emotionally beat up and the only thing that was safe was my family, but at that moment, no one felt safe. It felt as if I was being rejected by my mom, like she was ashamed of me, and therefore, I should feel ashamed of my scars. It was not until later in life when I came to the realization that she was trying to protect me from the possibility of people insulting me or staring at me.

I was hurt, but in my way of self-preservation, I pretended that it had not impacted me. As the summer months approached, I had purchased 2 bathing suits; a bikini and a one piece. At that time in my life, I myself was unsure which I was more comfortable with. My first reaction was to hide my scars, just as my mom taught me. But my deviant, 20-something attitude said, "If my mom has a problem, it's her hang up, not mine." As I showed my parents both suits I had purchased, my mom, as I expected, felt the one piece was more appropriate in public. But my dad, surprisingly, voted for the bikini, he said, "who cares if anyone is looking." From that day on, I never wore a one piece bathing suit again.

December of the year 2005 was a year that I was afraid would never come. I was graduating with a Bachelor's degree in Psychology from the University of Arizona. It had taken me 10 years of fighting against all odds to complete my education. I refused to let my health be the reason that my dreams never came true. It was like I was giving the middle finger to all of the Doctors that had told me to quit and file for disability. It was a special day and all of my family came to Tucson to show their support. It was the happiest time I could remember in years.

Some people think about their lives as a time line or on a continuum. Other people divide up their lives or compartmentalize them. These little building blocks of time form a person's lifespan. Some may form their building blocks by age divisions such as birth to age 30, 30 through age 60 and then 60 to death. Another person may find their building blocks are arranged more by where they lived. As a person ages, these sections of a life can almost feel like separate lifetimes. My building blocks seem to be defined by medical procedures as well as physical space and time. I had ended an era in my life; I was now ready to leave that behind and move forward.

I knew that I had been through the challenges of my life for a reason; I just was not sure what that reason was. One thing was certain, I wanted to help people, be an advocate for those suffering. I applied and was accepted to a graduate program in Irvine, California, for Marital and Family Therapy. I was ready to leave my past behind in Arizona and move onto the next era of my life.

Chapter 7:
Dating and Disease

August 13th, 2008 my first official date with Jason. He was so cute in those glasses!

*L*iving in California was unbelievable, how could it not be? I was living in the happiest place in the world, home of Disneyland. I couldn't wait to start school and find ways to get involved in the community. I began working as a manicurist at *St. Regis Hotel* in Dana Point and had a solid group of good friends. The California weather was perfect, and there was always something to get into. I met a girl named Casey at work and we quickly became friends. We decided to move into a condo together, and at the time, I had no clue that I was going to enter the happiest time in my single life. We made plans to go out and have fun almost every night, and the evenings when we did not have the energy to doll ourselves up for a night of craziness, we would spend it at home together in our pajamas with a cup of tea.

I felt that if I could exercise regularly, and stay busy, illness would not come knocking at my door. I began to notice that the left side of my body felt heavy after I fatigued my muscles at the gym. After a session with my personal trainer, I would find my body stiff and hard to move, but only on my left side. I would be able to relax the tension if I focused on but it would immediately go right back once I was distracted by something else. I would joke and called it my "lame lefty". I felt that if I named it, I would own it, like "Steve the Stoma" and then I could overcome it. I brought it up to my physician, but it was shrugged off as a result of pushing my body too far in the gym.

I kept my focus strong and graduated with my Master's Degree in Martial and Family Therapy. It was such an accomplishment, and I was ecstatic to start my internship at Phoenix House. I dedicated all of my time and energy into my future and tried not to look back. Casey, my adorable roommate, had been dating a Marine named Klein that was stationed at Camp Pendleton and wanted me to join them for dinner at Outback Steakhouse. I had gone to classes in the morning and then had been seeing clients all afternoon into the evening. The only thing I wanted to do was to throw my hair into a pony tail, kick off my high heels and eat a bowl of cereal, but Casey always had a way of persuading me to go out and have fun

I had to work late, so I arrived at the restaurant after they had ordered dinner. I said my hello's to my roommate and her boyfriend while noticing a cute man with adorable glasses. He introduced himself as Jason, a Marine from Kentucky, and his accent was intriguing. Noticing his full plate I asked him, "Why are you not eating?" He responded, "I had a big lunch" as he pushed his plate towards me, "Want some chicken?" I smiled and shook my head.

We made casual conversation during dinner and I later found out that Jason had already had eaten lunch at the same Outback Steakhouse that we were at, just four hours earlier. He received a call from Klein, telling him that he had to come to dinner and meet me that evening. Even though his stomach was full from just eating, he wanted to hang around to meet me, which I found charming.

As the evening progressed I found out that Jason was just coming back from his second tour in Iraq, had two siblings, liked reading books, and was ten years younger than me; yes, that was not a misprint, ten years younger than me! So that meant, when I was graduating high school, he was eight years old and don't forget that he also missed growing up in the 80's (which was an awesome decade). After we finished dinner, and Jason had shoveled a second meal down his throat, we all decided to go back to our condo to dive into the pool.

Casey and Klein found their way to the pool, and Jason and I were getting into to the hot tub. As Jason was taking his shirt off to get into the water he said, "I hope you like tattoos", referring to the multitude of artwork covering his chest and back. I grinned and said, "I hope you like scars," as I took off my towel covering the bikini my mother didn't want me to purchase. We both laughed and got into the water.

When we got back to the condo, I had a paper for school that I needed to finish on my laptop. Sitting on the couch next to me, Jason talked and flipped through the television channels as I was typing my paper. I noticed that he could not stop talking. Every channel that he came to, he would tell me little factoids about animals, science and commercials. I know that some people might have found it irritating, but I thought it was cute. That evening, I gave Jason the nickname "Wiki", because he was like a human Wikipedia. Anything that you were interested in learning about, he knew random facts and details about. I was actually pretty impressed by the amount of knowledge he could spew out.

As the night went on, Klein and Casey drank a little bit too much wine and decided to go to sleep. The only catch was now Jason was stuck at our condo because they had driven together. Being the nice host I am, I offered my bed so he could spend the night. We had a line of pillows right down the middle of the bed to keep our sleeping in the same bed platonic. After chatting for a while, I began to tell Jason my boundaries; I said, "Now, just so you know, I am not looking for a relationship. I am not going to be anyone's girlfriend; I am not your baby. I am right now focusing all my attention on my internship, but if you would like to be friends, I am open to that." I felt so proud of myself for setting rules. Little did I know that night I had met my future husband; Jason and I exchanged our vows six months later.

Everyone thought that we were crazy. We had just met and making such a huge commitment was scary, but for some reason I knew that it was the right choice for us. We had decided to get married at the Santa Ana Courthouse and would later, during the summer, have a reception when all of our family could attend. It was very romantic because it was just the two of us when we exchanged our vows on December 18th, 2008. That evening, Casey had put together an amazing mini-wedding reception at our condo for our local friends. I could not ask for anything more perfect! Although it was an exciting time in my life, I felt almost a little sad and scared to leave my single life with Casey behind.

As we began our new life together, we knew that we had to find a way to support ourselves financially. I had been promoted to the Admissions Coordinator at the Phoenix House which meant that I was responsible for interviewing, assessing, transporting, and admitting people needing residential care for substance abuse. Although I had never used drugs recreationally, I could relate to the feeling of using medications to help get through the emotional pain. It was a time when I was just finding myself and realizing what I could achieve when I had the opportunity to spread my wings.

Jason decided that he was going to start the application process to get onto the police force. I was so impressed by his determination. When Jason decides to do something, he will fully commit to the process, sometimes so dedicated that he pushes me out so he can focus on his goal. He flew through all the stages of the interviewing process and was one of only four men picked to go to the police academy for the City of Orange. I was proud of him. He would get up at 4:30 am every morning to go to the academy; he would be there until around 5 pm, come home and then do homework the rest of the night. It was a strain on our marriage, but I knew that it was only for 6 months, or so I thought.

We had just gotten our first apartment together in Orange. I felt that I began to fit into this world again as I started to get bothered by the little things, like going to the grocery store or cleaning. In the past, I would not have time to dwell on these details; when it is a life or death matter, you don't really care who took the garbage out last. We had purchased a dog together, Bella our Basset Hound, and I began to nest in our new home.

As Jason progressed though the academy, we began to argue more often. Up to this point, I never even knew that he was capable of yelling. I was shocked to find out that he would yell at me. In my family, if my Dad was angry, he would not talk to you. In fact, that is how you knew that you were in trouble, he was silent. His silence was deafening and way more upsetting then being shouted at. It was painful just to know that your Dad was disappointed in you.

When I have a couple come into therapy session, I usually hear the husband say, "She holds onto each word I say and she won't drop it. It is like she can remember every sentence, tone and detail from fights even years ago." I wish I could say that women do not have that ability, but I remember the very first time Jason said something rude to me. We had just moved into our new apartment and he had this huge big screen television and gaming system. It seems to be a staple in many men's lives. It does not matter if they have a futon in their living room and a week old box of pizza next to empty beer bottles. In the corner you will see a stack of egg crates holding up the pride of that man's life. Regardless of if they might have dug their furniture out of the trash, they will have a big flat screen television and some sort of gaming system that costs hundreds of dollars.

Jason and I were going to walk the dog to get the mail and I wanted to send back the rented movie that we had watched the night before. I have not had a lot of experience with video games since my 6th grade candy bar accomplishment so I had no clue how to get the DVD out of the vicious Play Station. I began pushing the lit buttons hoping that it would spit out the disk. Jason began to get impatient as he barked instructions at me while holding the dog's leash, "Not that button...it is not that difficult." I was getting upset as I felt my face getting flush with anger. I said, "I can't get it. Can you just walk over and help me?" Without missing a beat, Jason responded, "You have a F**king Master's Degree and you can't figure out how to get the DVD out of the Play Station?"

My jaw dropped to the floor. I could not believe that the man that I loved could even say those hurtful words to me. It does not matter that this fight happened years ago; still to this day, I can hear those words in my head and the pain it brought. I responded without thinking and chucked my keys at his head. This marked the beginning of almost a year of fights, arguments and spending a lot of time walking the dog alone.

I tried to keep myself busy to distract from the tension in my marriage. I enjoyed staying active, and although I did notice that my left side was slowing me down, I refused to believe that it was serious. During this time, I was visiting doctors and trying out various medications when the words Parkinson's disease (PD) came into my vocabulary. I, like many people, only knew of the illness from actor Michael J. Fox, who was diagnosed with young onset PD. My neurologist recommended that we follow the treatment for this disorder and I was willing to try anything that could help.

Usually Doctors will start off with a line of medications called Dopamine Agonists. Losing the medical lingo, I describe the medication like an imposter. It gets into our blood stream and tries to trick ourbodies into thinking that it is the chemical Dopamine that our bodies are losing due to Parkinson's disease. Mirapex is a type of medication in this category, which I was placed on for a little over six months. I was warned to watch for negative side effects such as excessive gambling, hyper-sexuality or other compulsive behavior.

I thought that it was a ridiculous to think that a person could develop these side effects. I have always been able to control urges and although my husband might not complain, hyper-sexuality just sounds like too much work. I began having hallucinations of creatures and children throughout my day. One afternoon, I was bringing my laundry from the patio when I heard someone coming up behind me at a fast pace. I dropped my laundry and prepared to protect myself, but no one was there. It was fascinating to me how real the hallucinations appeared.

One evening, Jason and I had ordered pizza (our favorite dish) and were watching a rented movie. We snuggled on my eggplant colored sofa. The movie was in full swing and had Jason's attention as he stared at the screen. Feeling the warmth of his body next to mine, I remember feeling for the first time in a long time, safe. I looked down at his hands that were entangled in mine and smiled. When the movie ended, we went to sleep, but my sleep was disrupted. I opened up my eyes as I felt a large weight on my body. There was a woman with long black hair sitting on my legs, with her back to me.

I tried to sit up but I could not move. I could not physically lift my legs. I began to sweat and thrash my body in different directions. I woke Jason up with my screaming as he turned on the lamp and grabbed me. My eyes adjusted to the burning of the light as I scanned the room. The woman was not there, but she was real to me. I was trying to explain what had happened but I knew how I must have sounded...crazy. The next day, I stopped taking Mirapex.

My body was deteriorating at an alarming rate and it was apparent that the medication was doing more damage than good. I had also not received the diagnosis of Parkinson's disease. The Doctors who were treating me did not want to give me such a detrimental diagnosis at a young age. There is no definitive test to see if you have Parkinson's or other neurological disorders. The best that can be done is to try various medications and track the symptoms and how they impact movement and gait. But my condition had begun to show itself in my cognitive functioning also.

Parkinson's disease is usually thought of as a movement disorder. This is because a person's movement issues can be easily observed, but to look inside their brain, to assess cognitive functioning, is a little bit more difficult. Another factor is that each individual is impacted by this condition in a different manner. We each have our own version of this illness. I have never had a tremor, but that is what people think of with PD. I am only symptomatic on my left side and sometimes get dystonia on my right foot. I am here to destroy any stigma that may come with PD.

Some people say to me "You don't look like you have Parkinson's disease." This makes me both laugh and want to punch someone in the face. I kindly say, "Thank you, I wear it well," with a smile. The truth of the matter is, no one can see inside my brain. They are just taking their prior misconception of PD and looking for physical symptoms. I have struggled much more with cognitive issues.

The part of the brain that controls executive functioning can be impacted by Parkinson's disease. This can be viewed like the "CEO" of a big company who is in charge of directing the organization of activities such as multitasking, solving problems, starting new tasks, and switching tasks. Language abilities can also be impaired; they include naming objects, generating words, comprehension, and verbal concepts. The most common language problem in PD is finding the "right" words. There is also a deficiency in memory function; people may find it difficult to concentrate on a conversation or reading a book. It may be challenging to talk to someone while walking and maintaining balance. Lastly, we have not even tapped into the mental aspects of the illness such a depression and anxiety. This is due to a chemical imbalance and medications can help.

I had heard that once Dopamine agonists were exhausted, the next step that Neurologists tend to take when trying to control movement disorders is moving to a category of medications which are combination of carbidopa and levodopa. This is typically in the form of a medication called Sinemet, which is like Dopamine in a pill. I was ready for the next step; although my hallucinations were spicing up my life, they honestly scared the hell out of me.

What is Parkinson's disease?

When you think of Parkinson's disease, what do you think of? Let me guess, a 60-ish year old man with a tremor? Have you ever thought it could be a 32 year old female with rigidity, slowness of movement, and cognitive issues? That is the stigma we face today. When you look up the definition of the illness, more or less, it is a movement disorder, but it goes so much deeper than that.

- Parkinson's disease is a chronic, degenerative neurological disorder that affects one in 100 people over age 60. While the average age at onset is 60, people have been diagnosed as young as 18.

- Research indicates that at least one million people in the United States, and more than five million worldwide, have Parkinson's, although this number is an estimate.

- An English doctor, James Parkinson, in 1817 was the first to categorize this illness. Today, we understand Parkinson's to be a disorder of the central nervous system that results from the loss of cells in various parts of the brain that produce dopamine, a chemical messenger responsible for transmitting signals within the brain that allow for coordination of movement. Parkinson's is one of several diseases categorized by clinicians as movement disorders. Recently, clinicians have begun examining the impact of Parkinson's on our cognitive functioning.

- Early symptoms are usually movement-related, including shaking, rigidity, slowness of movement and difficulty with walking and gait. Later, cognitive and behavioral problems may arise, with dementia commonly occurring in the advanced stages of the disease. Other symptoms include sensory, sleep, and emotional problems.

- There is no blood test or brain scan to make a diagnosis of Parkinson's. Instead, a doctor takes a careful medical history and performs a thorough neurological examination, looking in particular for two or more of the cardinal signs to be present. These signs are resting tremor, slowness of movement, balance problems, and rigidity. Frequently, the doctor will also look for responsiveness to Parkinson's medications as further evidence that Parkinson's is the correct diagnosis.

- As of today, there is no cure for Parkinson's disease. Treatment is limited to medications and various surgical procedures which may slow the progression of the illness.

- Exercise is crucial to achieving optimal health and even more important for people with Parkinson's disease. With a proper balance, fitness can be beneficial to individuals that are struggling with life cycle changes such as a new diagnosis of a physical ailment and the stress that is placed on the body due to these challenges. Studies confirm the benefit of exercise improves not only physical health and overall well-being, but can further alter one's emotional state. Approximately 40% of Parkinson's patients suffer from depression. What does this all mean? Integrating fitness into your daily routine can not only improve your symptoms, but can also keep the dark clouds of depression away.

Chapter 8:
Life, Love and Parkinson's

Our wedding reception in June 2009.

*J*ason and I had begun to live parallel lives. His life was absorbed in the police force and as I have stated, when he sets his mind to something, he can single focus on the task at hand to such an extent that he can push me out. I found ways to keep myself busy with work, sometimes working six days a week. I would work all hours of the day. Sometimes I would have a client being released from incarceration at two in the morning, and I enjoyed having such a positive impact on other people's lives. I would follow an individual from interviewing and assessing them in custody and then weeks or months later completing the admission process. I began to meet families and friends that were impacted by addiction, and I wanted to help.

Fitness had been such a positive experience in my life. I knew that finding healthy alternatives to using drugs could potentially help my clients. I began to create a program in my head that could provide fitness activities to the community regardless of agility or income. With the help of National Academy of Sports Medicine (NASM) I became a certified personal trainer and launched a fitness program at the Phoenix House called "Fit for Recovery" in August of 2009. This was the first time as an adult that I saw my true potential. I single handedly coordinated events, guest fitness classes and field trips. The relationships that I had created helped me secure a donation from a 24 Hour Fitness gym that was closing its doors. With 17 pieces of fitness equipment, the residents now had a gym to help maintain their new habits.

Although I was excelling professionally and making a difference in people's lives, my marriage had begun to take a negative turn. I used the experiences of my job to gain the praise and support I needed in life. Jason was rarely home and when he was, we argued. We had begun to see a therapist in hopes of saving the marriage. Ironically, we were fighting so much because we missed each other and never got to spend any time together without the distraction of our work. We were holding our wedding reception for our families and friends. I knew that I would be meeting his family from Mt. Sterling, Kentucky, which made me a little nervous. How could I pretend that we had a great marriage and that we were happy? I love Jason with all of my heart but our lives were in competition. Our personal morals and beliefs were also in opposition. As he locked people up for breaking the law, I was on the other end, releasing them.

I was taking Sinemet five to six times a day and barely controlling my symptoms. I could hardly keep up with my normal gym regimen. I had begun to assist my left arm and leg during my daily activities, which was alarming, because my body just did it without me thinking about it. I began to trip and drag my left leg but that was not the only thing I noticed; my left arm did not swing when I walked. If I consciously thought about swinging my arm, I could, but the moment I got distracted it would just hang there limp and dead. I had done much research on my own about Parkinson's disease and felt that although it was unlikely, the symptoms described on the internet sounded just like my lame lefty.

I can remember the day that my fear became a reality. I sat in an uncomfortable flower-print chair in my neurologist's office. The nurses in the front office were talking to each other about what type of sandwiches they would order for lunch. The background was filled with traces of annoying soft-rock music and an overpowering smell of coffee. It was apparent that someone put much effort into creating a calm and relaxing environment, but at the moment it felt as irritating as wearing an itchy sweater in the desert.

A nurse came into the waiting area and called my name. I followed the nurse as she guided me to the exam room. Hearing the diagnosis — "You have Parkinson's disease. There is no cure, and you will struggle with this the rest of your life." — was like being punched in the stomach. I felt cheated out of a life that held so much promise. I looked down at my rigid left arm, resting lifeless on my lap. It felt alien. This was not the same arm that helped me make the cheerleading squad. These were not the fingers that I used to play the flute in my high school band.

I was angry, sad, and scared. You can prepare for a new job, a baby, or a tropical vacation. But there's nothing you can do to prepare to watch your body deteriorate at the age of 32. I was shocked by how fast my disease progressed. Looking into the mirror every morning became the biggest challenge of the day. The expressionless face that stared back at me seemed unfamiliar. I felt damaged. Walking was starting to become a struggle. I feared that anyone who saw what I had become might pity me or look down on me. So I spent every day trying to hide my diagnosis from the world — even from my husband, Jason.

My body moved slowly through my morning rituals. When I tried to button my shirt, I got frustrated that my fingers couldn't seem to figure it all out. I was just about to yell something vulgar when I heard my husband coming up the stairs. A wave of panic rushed over me. How was I going to hide this?

Up to this point, I had found some absurd explanation for every awkward symptom of my young-onset Parkinson's disease. When Jason entered the room, I swung around with a smile, as if I had intentionally left my shirt unbuttoned for him. He grinned back, and I felt relieved that I had averted another possible disaster. Then I realized that the disaster was not the disease or its symptoms but the fact that I was trying to hide who I really was. All the energy I spent trying to cover up my illness had drained me.

I could not keep this from the man that I loved anymore. I sat my husband on the couch and tried to explain what Parkinson's disease was. It was my "CliffsNotes" version, direct and to the point. After spilling my well-rehearsed speech, I took a breath and waited for his reaction. He just stared at me with a confused look on his face and said, "Um, I knew you had Parkinson's disease."

I began to cry. All the days I spent trying to be perfect were for nothing. The man I had tried to protect from the devastating effects of my illness had known my secret all along. "My disease won't go away," I blurted out. "It will only get worse, and I don't want you to see me or remember me like this. I don't want to burden you!" Jason looked at me and calmly said, "A burden is something that is placed on you, not something that you choose." He had chosen to be with me, Parkinson's or not. The burden was the fear I had placed on myself.

I was coming to the realization that the very fact I had Parkinson's disease was just as hard on me as it was on my family and friends. I had visited my parent's in Mesa; I knew telling them in person was the best. We were standing in their kitchen with the hum of the dishwasher in the background. I detailed the symptoms of my illness and the diagnosis from my physicians. My father just nodded but did not say a word. I said, "I just can't believe how fast it is progressing. I feel hopeless, like no one is taking me serious." My Dad turned his head and began to weep. Through his tears, he said, "It is just not fair. You have been through so much." When my mom and I noticed, we all began to bawl. The only time I had seen my Dad cry is when my grandmother Betty passed away when I was a little girl. Until that day, I never fully understood how much my health had impacted my family.

I had an extremely hard time accepting it and that was partly due to the reaction from other people. I would constantly hear, "You don't look like you have Parkinson's disease" or "You don't have a tremor like my grandpa did." As if you have to look bad or worse than you feel inside. It is just like someone saying you are crazy, that you seem normal, when you feel like you are spiraling out of control. I knew that the only way I was going to get the help I needed, was if I started doing the work. I began researching the history of Parkinson's and the details of the illness. I even began calling myself a "Parkie". It did not make sense to use the word disease. I was not infecting anyone. I am not contagious.

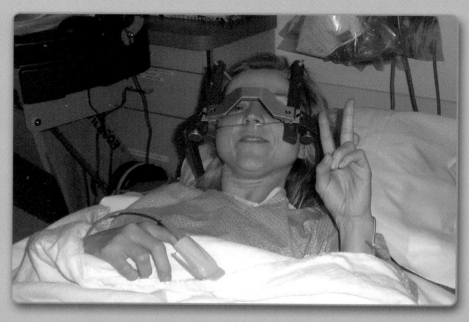

April, 2010 wearing my halo during my first Deep Brain Stimulation Surgery.

I had heard about a surgery called Deep Brain Stimulation (DBS) to help control the symptoms of Parkinson's. I wanted to learn more about the procedure, so I located the Physician known for his extensive work in implanting these units in Newport Beach, California. Little did I know I was about to meet the man that would ultimately change my life forever, Dr. Christopher Duma. I sat in the waiting area of the Neurosurgeon and tried to occupy my thoughts with something other than the fear of getting my brain operated on. Looking around the room, I saw a stack of magazines and a bowl of candy resting on a coffee table. Why is it that at any physician's office you will find the magazine "Highlights"? It is almost like the Doctors send each other memos about the latest issue and answers to the crossword puzzles.

I hear a female voice say, "Allison, can I get a copy of your insurance card?" Turning towards the sound of the voice I see the top of the receptionist's head as she is looking down. I picked up my purse and approach the window. If there is anyone who should teach a class in multi-tasking, it is these ladies in the Doctor's office. Without lifting her head and while continuing her conversation on the phone, she reached for my card. She pushed herself off the desk and rolled over to the copy machine.

As she scanned my insurance card, I could hear her say, "I know Mr. Jones, but the Doctor cannot see you this week, I am going to have to refer you to the emergency room." I wondered what Mr. Jones was going through and how frustrated he must be by just getting the brush off in his time of need. The receptionist scuttled back to the open window and handed me my card without saying a word to me or even looking at me as she continued to fail miserably at calming Mr. Jones on the other line. I looked at the candy on the table and grabbed an oversized handful of tootsie rolls. Here I was waiting to talk to a person about getting my head cut into, and God knows what poor Mr. Jones was facing, and this woman appeared to be just going through her daily tasks with no emotion. I wanted to chuck my delicious treats at her, but I really did

75

not want to waste a perfectly good tootsie roll.

A cheerful nurse appeared in the doorway and called my name. I stood up and followed her down the hallway to Dr. Duma's office. He has a cozy corner office and a couch that you could melt into. He introduced himself, but I had already heard about the amazing work he does. He has removed tumors and helps people that have had a stroke. I was in the presence of a true hero. As he sat behind his gigantic oak desk, wearing a white lab coat he smiled as he read my medical file. He was probably thinking in his head, "I got this."

Dr. Duma went on to tell me that DBS was a possibility and that it could increase the amount of time my medications were working all while lowering the amount of Dopamine I currently had to take each day. I felt apprehensive; I had felt hopeless, it couldn't be this easy. He detailed the surgery, "We break the surgery up into three procedures with one week intervals. We make a small incision on your hair line, and place the lead. You will be awake so we can make sure that we have the correct location to give you the best results with few side effects." I felt nauseous. He continued explaining as the big screen behind him turned on and began playing a video. His words began meshing together and my vision got blurry as I began to cry.

I had so much running through my head. Would I have to shave some of my hair? Just like many woman, my hair was a huge part of who I was, and I could not imagine losing even small patches! Dr. Duma assured me that he completely understood my fear and had perfected, using the natural growth of his patient's hair, a small incision that would not affect my current hair style. I know that it may seem vain, but hey, I am still a young woman!

I was also afraid of more scars. How huge are these stimulators that are going into my chest? I had just accepted my tummy scars and my determination not to let it impact my bikini choices, but now I would be sentenced to a life of turtlenecks? Without missing a beat, Dr. Duma informed me that he could do a special placement of the stimulators going in through my armpits and placing them under my breast tissue. This way, I would still be able to wear clothing of my choice, without fear of people noticing my electrical enhancements.

I could not process the probability that this surgery was going to happen. I had been through hell and now this. I was bitter and resentful. I had made a new life for myself, and once again, my health tripped me. I cannot remember my response to Dr. Duma, I just remember putting my sunglasses on and grabbing another handful of tootsie rolls as I walked through the waiting room. I reached for the door, feeling the cold metal of the handle; I glanced back at the receptionist who was still on the phone. I felt annoyed that she could not feel my pain; I was once again, alone.

I had an appointment to take a test called the "Sinemet Challenge". I was to stop taking my medications the night before, so the Doctor could see what my movement was like with no support from medication. Then I would take my medication, and after an hour re-do, the test. This would allow for a proper diagnosis and the proper treatment.

I decided to start filming my adventure through the Parkinson's world with hope that maybe it could help someone else know what this experience was like. The morning of my "Sinemet Challenge," I gripped my camera in my unsteady hand and I looked into the mirror. I noted my left arm was not moving when I walked; it just hung there like a dead tree branch, as I zoomed in on myself. I do have to admit, the best part of that one minute video was my amazing hair. It was freakishly beautiful that day. Maybe it knew the emotional wreck my mind was in; my hair thought the least it could do was to be on its best behavior.

As Jason and I drove to Dr. Duma's office, I just stared out the car window. I had become numb. My body was rigid and moving was painful, but sitting still felt like being stuck with pins and needles. I keep thinking of my favorite quote "This too shall pass" but in that moment, I felt that I was stuck in a life I had not been promised. Just like one of those dreams you get when you cannot move fast enough and something horrible is chasing you. My feet were stuck in a huge pile of honey, and there was no hope that I would ever move again.

When we got to the office, we were guided back to an exam room with a Physician's Assistant (PA) holding a video camera. I was directed to do standard movements that could be challenging to someone with Parkinson's. I was asked to tap my fingers together, and in my mind, it did not seem unreasonable. I did the movement in my right hand as the PA recorded me. I switched sides to do the exact same thing on my left hand, but I could not replicate the movement. I stared at my left hand and focused. It took all of my brain power to slowly tap my fingers. I was shocked at how bad I was without medication. I fought the urge to cry. "Pull it together Allison, you have been through worse," I thought to myself. After completing the test, Jason and I slowly walked back to the car in silence. I could not fight it anymore; tears began streaming down my face.

It did not take long to decide to do the surgery; I was willing to try anything that might slow my illness down. I called and talked to my parents about my decision. I explained to them, "The main concept of Deep Brain Stimulation (DBS) is that I will have stimulators placed in my chest and a wire will run from that unit to the leads that are implanted in my brain. These leads will give me a continuous dose of electrical current to my brain to stimulate the creation and efficient use of Dopamine. I will be awake during the procedures, so I can communicate with Dr. Duma to ensure that the leads are in the correct geographical locations in my brain." As I heard the description coming out of my mouth, it sounded totally creepy. I could only imagine what my parents were thinking.

The one thing that kept running through my head was how technology had come so far. It amazed me. The fact that someone even thought about running wires into the brain and then sending electrical current, was unsettling to me. Could you imagine being the first patient to receive this? I envisioned a doctor with a cord from a lamp and a battery pack telling a patient, "Don't worry about a thing! We are going to send electrical current through this wire into your brain and rig you up to a battery, but we have a really good feeling that this will work!"

I did my best in trying to prepare myself and my work for the upcoming DBS surgery. April 22nd, 2010 I had my first brain surgery. I had the normal butterflies, but as we got closer to starting, they turned into bats flopping around in my tummy. The first part of the surgery is the placement of the head frame. They gave me some Propofol so I would not remember it, which was great since I would have sold my toes for the opportunity to forget my pain.

As I came to, I was on a gurney and unable to lift my head; the weight of the halo was heavy. My parents and Jason came in to help ease my nerves. We took some pictures and chatted for a bit but the pain from the metal pins holding my halo was becoming unbearable. Then out of the corner of my eye, I saw the nurses leaning in towards each other and whispering, "Dr. Duma is here." You would think that by the way they were talking, my Neurosurgeon should be floating in on a cloud with sun rays beaming off of his flesh as angels sing his praise.

Dr. Duma rounded the corner in a full suit and jacket. I was a little thrown off by his attire. I thought to myself, "He is totally going to wear that into surgery. He is known as the top DBS surgeon in Southern California, who's going to tell him no." He introduced himself to my parents, and we said our goodbyes. It does not matter how many damn surgeries I have endured, I always have a thought in the back of my head, "What if this is the last time I see my family."

The next thing I remember vaguely is waking up in the surgery room and being told to do certain movements by the Physician's Assistant. I could feel that my head was secured by something, but I was unable to see above my eyebrows. Then I was asked to count backwards in increments of 7 from 100. I thought about it and then said "100...93...ummmm...I can't even do this when I am awake." Everyone was laughing in the operating room when all of the sudden, my body relaxed. It was a sensation that is hard to describe. Imagine tensing all of your muscles and then relaxing them; my rigidity just disappeared. They were stimulating the right area; they had found the perfect spot to place the lead. I shouted, "That's it!" There were giggles and conversations around me but I could not recognize all the voices. I was sedated again and woke up to my husband in the recovery room. I thought "I did it! I made it through my first surgery."

My parents were staying in Orange County for a few days just so my mom could make massive amounts of food and clean our apartment. Those days are a little foggy, but I do remember that I could not wash my hair for 72 hours due to my incisions. By the third day, I could have sworn that a family of birds had been nesting in my hair by the amount of oil, dried blood and other shenanigans. My mom offered to help me wash my hair before my parents left to go back to Mesa, Arizona.

My mom has this amazing ability to push all of her emotions aside and focus on the medical task at hand. She made me a little seat by the bathtub and had me lean forward as she used the shower hose to begin the decontamination process. The water was warm against my scalp, but very calming. We sat in silence as my mom put shampoo into her hands and then gently began to wash my hair. The smell of the fragrant bubbles awakened me. It was a moment that will be with me forever. The comfort of her touch always made illness a little easier to handle.

On April 19th, 2010, the other side of my head was operated on. Knowing the routine made some of the anxiety a little less impactful. Everything went as planned, and I woke up with a total of 34 staples, ear to ear. That was a little bit more invasive then "just a small incision on your hairline" as Dr. Duma explained. I was bruised all down my neck and very sore, but ready to get home to heal. I knew that my job at Phoenix House was challenged by my absence, although they were determined to let me have time to recover. I was always the one wanting to go back to work earlier than people would like.

I woke up excited the morning of my third surgery on May 6th, 2010. I was ready to be done with all this hospital crap and wanted to get back to a somewhat normal life. As I sat in the waiting area, I began to get nervous. I could barely sit still as I bounced around in my chair. I heard my name called and I stood up to walk back to the surgery prep room. I got changed into my fashionable, yet functional hospital gown and took seat on my bed. At this point in my life, I knew the routine of preparing for surgery like I was an operating room nurse.

The Anesthesiologist introduced himself, but I was so anxious I could not remember his name. Trying to get an I.V. started was not a walk in the park either. They tried to secure a line 6 times, including my foot, just to realize I had no veins left that were able to be used. The Anesthesiologist decided to have me breathe in Nitrous Oxide, which would put me to sleep, so they could dig with a needle in my arm to get a vein. But in order to do this, I had to be wheeled into the operating room completely awake.

As I lay on my back on a gurney, I was rolled into a small room full of people dressed in scrubs. I gazed at the prep table that was organized methodically with shiny, cold metal surgical equipment. I looked at the operating table. It was then that the surgery became real. I began to break down as my eyes started to water. They prepped my body for surgery and gave me a mask to hold onto my face and directed me to begin to take deep breaths. The medical team scurried around my operating table, almost in a rhythmic dance, for each one knew their assigned task at hand. As my body felt calm and relaxed, my mind had a totally different emotion....fear.

The anesthesiologist had me hold on to the mask, I am assuming to gauge when I was losing consciousness. I felt the plastic of the mask pressing up against my face, which had a vague scent of strawberries. I did as I was told, and focused on deep breaths, terrified knowing that the air I was inhaling would ultimately put me under sedation, which also had a deeper meaning of not being in control of my own body. They would ask me questions, "Are you still there Allison?" I had a delayed response...but I continued to talk.

I felt the strength in my hand starting to weaken. I was unable to muster any pressure to hold the plastic mask, and my hand began to slip. I could hear the beeping of the machines....pumping fluid into my body (which meant that they had got a vein) and I knew that it was ok to let go because they had found I.V. access. But I was terrified to let go of the mask, so I continued to press it hard against my face.

I gripped onto the edges of the strawberry scented mask, fighting to stay conscious and then my hand began to give. I heard a nurse say, "Here she goes." She held my other hand to offer some sort of comfort and as I gripped the fingers of a stranger, I said, "I am scared to go."...now whether or not that was in my head...I am unsure. But my fear and desperation of not letting go was apparent to the whole room of medical professionals.

The anesthesiologist said to me "It is alright to let go.....we have you.....you are in good hands." My whole life up to this point has been not to let go; to fight with every ounce of my being to live. Hearing the words, "let go" triggered my inner fear of dying and I began to sob uncontrollably. I felt the hands of the nursing staff on my shoulder as my body trembled...and I let go...

Later that evening, I was eating my delicious "In-N-Out" Burger with my salty fries at our dinner table. I was drained from my procedure I had that day, so I topped my meal with a chocolate milkshake. I was half-way through my feast when out of nowhere I just started crying. With a mouth full of burger, hot tears began streaming down my face. I look at that moment as if my body were a closet. As I collected stuff from my day, I shoved it into my closet, but every time I went to shove something else in it, stuff fell out on me.

Everything that I had gone through that day that I just kept pushing down, just trying to survive, came out of me through my tears. I welcomed the release. Jason stared at me with a bewildered look on his face as the trauma of my emotional and physical pain, began the adventure of leaving my body. Jason had not a clue what to do and I could feel his anger and frustration. He said, "Why are you crying"? I just quietly muttered, "You do not have to fix anything, just let me have a minute."

As I have found out during this ordeal, Jason does not feel comfortable around emotions or tears. If he cannot find a solution to make me stop crying, he becomes irritated. This does not come from him being insensitive to my feelings, but I believe that this comes from the desire to take away my pain. If he is unable to construct a resolution to my agony, he feels he has failed as a husband.

After my incisions had time to heal, I was scheduled to visit Dr. Kenneth Martinez, M.D. neurologist and movement disorder specialist. The correct placement of the leads in my brain was just as crucial as the programming of the stimulators. Dr. Martinez explains, "A good analogy for the postoperative management of DBS is that it is a lot like adjusting a radio. The first steps when turning the DBS device 'on' involve mapping the right locations along the metal lead/wire that work the best for each individual patient. This is like selecting the correct radio station on the dial or finding the right type of 'music' your brain prefers. Does it prefer classical, jazz, rock & roll, or hip-hop?" I giggled and said, "I hope it is not mariachi music! That would definitely keep me up at night!"

Dr. Martinez had such a talent for simplifying the overwhelming medical terminology. Jason found his chance to lighten the tone of the room as he piped in, "Can you program her to be a better cook?" We all began to laugh as I hit him in the chest. I said, "Hey now, I can order a mean pizza!" Dr. Martinez continued, "Once we have found the best 'station' that causes your brain to respond optimally, we need to set the 'bass', 'treble' and 'volume' just like on a regular radio. They are infrequently adjusted (just like the bass and treble) and often have standard settings for Parkinson's that we start with based on the location of the lead in the brain."

I questioned, "Does my radio station ever change?" He responded, "Once these are set, we finally slowly ramp up on the 'volume' -voltage until we arrive at a 'comfortable listening level' which would provide optimal relief of the Parkinson's symptoms. Over time with disease progression, we may need to turn up the voltage to relieve worsening Parkinson's symptoms just as you would have to turn up the volume on the radio to hear it equally well as your hearing declines with age. It also avoids the incorrect and oversimplified concept of: DBS is a light switch - turn it on and everything is better immediately." I thanked him for his time with a smile. He put my mind at ease taking the fear and unknown out of the programming of DBS.

With the right radio station programmed, I was ready to tackle to world again. Not only was my movement improving, but my cognitive functioning was coming back. I was ready to jump back into life. When my friends would see me, they would say, "You look great! You can't even tell you had anything done." I knew that they were not just saying this to be kind. It was true! I did not have the standard devil horns, which are from the leads sticking out of your skull slightly. Dr. Duma had pioneered a skill that shaves the skull down so the leads are flush with your scalp. But the most amazing thing was the wire going down my neck did not look like an alien baby, it looked like I had just had a killer session at the gym and my veins were all pumped up! Not a bad look!

One of the wonderful symptoms of having this disease is that each day, I never know how I will feel. Some days I have energy and passion to tackle the day and some days I have the "blahs". My definition of the "blahs" are days when you don't feel good, and just the thought of getting up out of bed makes you say "blah". I try to push the "blah" clouds away as much as I can, but those storms seem to sneak in when I am not paying attention. Parkies can never recreate a good day. Even if I eat the same food, do the same activities, or even wear the same clothes, I am still at the mercy of my condition.

One day I was in the kitchen cooking one of my husband's favorite dishes, pasta and breaded chicken. The steam from the boiling water on the stove was rising from its pot. I had all the ingredients spread out onto the counter as I bopped around the kitchen in a cheerful mood. I grasped the jar of marinara sauce and began to twist off the lid. I felt my face get warm as I began to struggle. The damn jar had no intentions of letting me enjoy its contents. I was growling as I began to shake from the amount of strength I was exuding, when Jason entered the room. I was angered by the fact that this container was laughing at me but I was even more irritated that Jason had not offered to help. I barked at him, "Well are you just going to walk by? Open this...." I shoved the jar in his face.

In retrospect, maybe not the best way to ask for help, but I was never good at telling someone I needed them. The next day, I was busy in the kitchen making a peanut butter and jelly sandwich, which in my opinion, is one of man's greatest inventions. Then it happened again, the damn jelly jar began to laugh at me. Taunting me, I thought about throwing it to the ground and breaking it, but that just seemed too sticky. Jason walked right over to me and reached out his hand to help. Without thinking, I took out all my PB and J resentment on him as I snapped, "I am not handicapped, I can get it." He just stared at me in amazement. This is how Parkinson's can change my mood day to day.

I loved my job at Phoenix House but now I was finding it hard to even multitask anymore. I couldn't tell if it was from the medications or the progression of my illness. It was not helpful that I had never even met anyone with Parkinson's because I did not have anyone to compare to. I started to seek other support groups in the area and decided to get involved. One of the fears that come with someone like me getting diagnosed at such a young age is that there are not many people that are young onset. I have not met anyone yet that is as young as I am. I have had conversations with a few, but it would be nice to have someone going through similar challenges.

Many young onset Parkies tend to not want to go to support groups, because they will be faced the reality of what they possible could look like. I, on the other hand, found it comforting. I did not have to worry about hiding my symptoms. I would listen to the challenges that others were facing due to Parkinson's. I also began to learn about little tips or the latest research for controlling my symptoms.

Chapter 10:
Strength in Pain

Date Night at the **Erase MS Gala**

I guess that it happens to everyone at some point in their life; when the family roles switch and children begin to take care of their parents. It is one of life's cruel jokes. The last few times I had called my Dad, he sounded sick but I just assumed it was just a bout of the flu not clearing up. You never think of your Dad being sick. My parents had come to visit and I was looking forward to seeing them.

Up to this point my mom had thought of every possible reason why my life of sickness was her fault, such as her inability to breastfeed for an extending length of time. Knowing deep in my heart that she would give her life if it would have made me healthy, I would make attempts to have her see that her way of thinking was ridiculous.

I have an obsession with handbags especially those made by Coach. One afternoon as we were shopping, we passed a window with beautiful leather purses. I said to my mom, "Do you see that purple leather tote?" She nodded. "A new study out shows that Coach purses raise Dopamine levels, but it is not FDA approved yet," I replied with grin. "It must be that you did not buy me enough bags when I was growing up to prevent me from getting Parkinson's disease," I said with a giggle. My mom chuckled and said, "Alright, alright...I get it."

On the last day of their visit, my parents wanted to talk with me over lunch. As we drove around in the testosterone oozing Ford Escape, my dad said, "My Doctor has done some tests and found something wrong with my blood. It is called, Myelodysplastic Syndrome. They feel that I may benefit from doing a mild dose of chemotherapy in a couple of months." I responded, "Didn't grandma die from Leukemia?" Dad nodded his head in agreement and replied, "Yes, but we don't need to worry about that right now." I was speechless. I looked at my mother in disbelief. I was stunned by how the tone of the conversation was so passive, it felt like we were talking about someone else; not my father.

After my parents drove home, I stayed focused on work, which had become a great coping mechanism. I knew that they were sugar coating my Dad's diagnosis, but it was frustrating that no one seemed to talk about the fact that Dad was ill. A few weeks later, I got an email from the social network "CarePages" and it noted that my Dad had requested me to join his blog. I clicked on the link and it directed me to the "CarePages: Leukemia and Lymphoma Society." I could not breathe as my father's face appeared on the computer screen.

That was the day that my world stopped turning. Gleaming on the screen was my Dad's community blog and the words "Blood Cancer". Everything went dark around me. I felt rage. The only word that I could bring into my head was "Why?" I had been dragged through purgatory and now the devil was coming for my family. I had already begun to accept that my life would be filled with illness, fear and pain, but not my Dad's. That night, after a long break from my spirituality, I got down on my knees in the middle of my living room and prayed.

Adjusting to my Dad's diagnosis was a struggle, especially since no one in my family was talking about it. When I would ask my Dad how he was feeling it was always, "Oh, I am doing alright. So did you watch *Dancing with the Stars* last night?" He thought that he was tricking me by the swift subject change, but he was awful at perfecting the skill. When I asked Mom how she was handling it, "Oh, your father is o.k., just a little tired." This left me to communicate with him and learn about his health on a community blog, just like his acquaintances did. He would post pictures of his chemotherapy treatment room and would joke and say that homemade oatmeal cookies were part of his treatment. In the therapy world, we have a saying that I like to live by, "we meet the client where they are at." This meant that if my Dad couldn't talk to me physically, I would meet him where he was at. Maybe he felt that if he said it out loud to his daughter, the diagnosis became real.

Normally when I have devastating news or need support, I would rely on my husband or call a friend. But this was different; I could not even say the words "Blood Cancer" without breaking down into tears. I wanted to talk about it and organize my thoughts, but I was unable to ask for help. I held onto anger and resentment. I had come to accept that my life would be crammed with medical procedures and tests. I had been preparing for this reality. I could handle it. I was built for it. Give me another illness to conquer, just let my Dad live a long healthy and happy life.

Preparing for his first dose of chemotherapy, I wanted to be there for him, just like he was for me. I decided that I would use social media and texting to communicate. It was easier for him to chat over text messages than on the phone. Then I explained to him using the keyboard of my smartphone, that in his attempt to protect me, he was hurting me. I needed to feel included. Then I had an epiphany. This was not about me! This was what my Dad was going through, and I had to respect his wishes. I just had to be there for him when he needed support. The next day, I made oatmeal cookies and mailed them to him.

Just so I don't keep you in suspense, my Dad later on, found out that he had been misdiagnosed. He did not have Myelodysplastic Syndrome, but in fact did have something called "Hairy Cell Leukemia", (ironic, seeing as my Dad is balding) which has a high success rate of remission. The Doctor prescribed him a new chemotherapy that requires a 24/7 infusion, but slowly he regained his strength. He has now returned to his position at the school district, and is back to his full-time job of being my Dad.

My job at Phoenix House was drawing to an end. Going through DBS surgery made me realize that I needed to slow down my frantic pace. Jason was working graveyard shifts, so we were just passing each other during the day, but not being able to fully connect. I had become so depressed. Just trying to function each day was becoming a struggle, but I had no one to tell this to. I felt that Jason would see me as weak if I told him how dark my life had become. So I held it in. One evening while Jason was working late, I thought to myself, "If I was gone, I wonder how long it would be before Jason noticed I wasn't here?" The thought was random, but scared me enough to know that we needed to make some drastic changes. If our marriage was going to survive, I would have to face the reality of depression and fear.

Over the last 8 years of my life, I had learned not to rely on anyone. I felt that it is when you need someone most, they will disappoint you. I loved Jason, but I did not want to ask him for help. I was a young, attractive, independent woman who could take care of herself, or so I thought. It was not until I became vulnerable in my marriage, that a shift began to dramatically change our relationship. I let him know how unhappy I was in life and if we were going to make it work, we had to make sacrifices. In October 2010, Jason left the police force and I gave my notice at the Phoenix House.

We decided to move into a new apartment in a completely different city, 15 miles away from our old lives. We were putting the final boxes into the moving truck when I walked back into the apartment to make sure nothing was left behind. Standing in the middle of our empty living room, I thought back to all the arguments and fights that occurred within those walls. I felt nauseous thinking of all the hurtful and mean comments that we had said to each other. I wanted to just run out of the apartment, but I knew that I had to leave something behind. I was going to leave all the negativity from our past in that apartment, I refused to pack it in a card board box and bring it into our new home.

We moved into a two bedroom apartment in Laguna Niguel, California. Before we left the City of Orange, we had adopted a puppy that was hit by a car outside of Phoenix House. We named him "Crash", which seemed appropriate because of the accident that had him crashing into our hearts. Jason had decided to go to the local community college and start working on his education. We had begun to look like a totally different couple. I no longer used an alarm clock and found it amusing to watch the traffic reports in the morning. Being honest, I was quietly laughing at all the cars stuck in rush hour traffic as I sat on my couch, drinking tea in my pajamas. Jason had begun wearing flip flops and jeans instead of polyester uniforms. He had also decided to stop wearing his military style haircut and let his hair grow.

We had gone from barely seeing each other to spending everyday with each other. But it was not just the outside appearance that made us different. We were becoming a couple again. Now when we would see our therapist, we would complain about the house not getting cleaned or other typical marital disagreements. I began to rely on him for strength and, although it was terrifying, I trusted that he would keep me safe. It was not until I could cry in front of him and tell him my fears that we could shape our relationship. I was going from a person not needing anyone, to needing and wanting him in my life. I started getting butterflies in my tummy when we would spend time with each other. I would catch myself just staring at him. I was falling in love all over again.

Chapter 11:
Parkinson's in Balance

Kevin Kwan

My attempt at squashing the politics in the Parkinson's community at the first annual Unity BBQ.
It didn't turn out as planned, but there is always next year!

I needed to find a new occupation, but one that could encompass the limitations my health can bring. I also wanted to continue on my path as a Marital and Family Therapist Intern working towards my licensure, but hopefully within the medical field. I wanted to feel passionate about my work, but the economy was making any employment challenging to find. I was beginning to see the gaps in the help offered to Parkies and their families and the limitations in support. I also found strength and happiness being in the company of those who could understand my pain. The light bulb went on. I could create a program that is just for those affected by Parkinson's disease. That is when my dream started to take form.

I wanted to create a program that focused on a balance of the mental and physical health by offering fitness classes, support groups, and psychotherapy to the community. The name "Parkinson's in Balance" seemed like a perfect description of my program's intentions. Understanding that most Parkies cannot work and may be on disability or retired, I needed to find a way to offer help for free. It did not make sense to limit support to only those who could afford it.

I also thought about what type of support I saw that was missing in the community, and what I would find useful being a patient myself. Just like many other illnesses, the mental health aspect was completely neglected. It was just not spoken about. No one asked me how I was doing emotionally, and no referrals were offered to seek support. It appeared that I was to just handle any emotional pain that I had on my own. Every medical professional was phenomenal in their area of expertise, but no one was looking at the continuation of care.

Exercise is a key component when trying to slow the progression of Parkinson's. Studies confirm the benefit of exercise improves not only physical health and overall well-being, but can further alter one's emotional state.

Although exercise does not stop the progression of PD, I knew it could help the symptoms from which many people suffer. Fitness can improve range of motion, lessen rigidity and increase flexibility; so I knew that incorporating exercise into my program was crucial to help create a balance.

Another neglected area was awareness and advocacy. There are so many amazing foundations out there that focus on worthy causes such as Cancer, Diabetes and Multiple Sclerosis. But when I began researching resources for Parkinson's, I found that there were only a handful of national foundations and even fewer community programs. Then I looked at advocacy. I want you to answer this question, "When you think of Parkinson's disease advocates, what names come to mind?" The first response I get from people is Michael J. Fox or Muhammad Ali. These men have done amazing things and have paved the road that I am traveling, but they are only human. How can they help everyone in need?

I also understood that people respond to different levels of support. Some of the young onset Parkies do not want to go to a traditional support group. They will sit in a circle of chairs, with their cup of coffee, introduce themselves and talk about how Parkinson's has destroyed their reality. It can be extremely depressing for a young-onset to walk into a senior center for a community Parkinson's support group and be surrounded by elderly people that have advanced symptoms. Some of those individuals would prefer a community fitness class, where they can casually ask the person next to them, "What medications do you take?" Then you have the early diagnosed that have not made their illness public. This is when individual or couples psychotherapy in a private office can be beneficial. Now that I had an idea, what did I do with it? How do I get funding?

I was visiting my Neurosurgeon, Dr. Christopher Duma for a follow up appointment when I proposed to him my vision; the creation of a program that would help people in the community here, at this moment. There is so much focus on the future such as research and finding a cure, but where's the support for us today? The national foundations have chapters located throughout most of the major cities that help provide support for various types of illnesses through support groups or community events. These foundations reach many people and do a phenomenal job at providing education and resources to the masses. But with all the money that is collected by fundraising, a large percentage goes back to the national level to be distributed throughout the country. My goal was to get more personal, (be out there in the trenches, so to speak) providing ideas, energy, and motivating people in our community. I wanted to be an advocate.

I decided that the best way to find funding is to talk to the professionals that are currently working with the illness. As I described my intentions and my goals to Dr. Duma, he sat in silence, just grinning. After I finished exposing the details of my business plan, I said, "Well what do you think?" He responded, "It sounds like you want to do something that you feel passionate about, something that you can go home at night and feel good about the work you have done." I nodded in disbelief. Dr. Duma knew exactly where my head and heart was it. That day, he took a chance on a girl with an idea and "Parkinson's in Balance" came to life. The Foundation for Neuroscience, Stroke and Recovery (FNSR), a non-profit organization that he was the president of took my program under their wing and gave me a year to make my dream a reality.

"Parkinson's in Balance" launched October, 2010. I had created fliers detailing our support groups and designed a website offering our resources. I had begun teaching my first Parkinson's fitness class at a local gym. I had four people in regular attendance who I had meet in past support groups. As I was teaching the class, it appeared that no one was enjoying the activity. I was thinking to myself, "They hate me!" But after the class, each participant approached me and thanked me for my time. They told me that it was a great class and they couldn't wait to do it again. I learned the lack of facial expressions was a symptom of PD; it is known as a Parkinson's mask. I was researching ways to slow the progression of the illness and learning more about myself.

My biggest challenge was getting the word out that my program even existed. I had been asked to have an interview, for our local paper, "The OC Register". It was going to be done by the reporter that had covered my Phoenix House "Fit for Recovery" program, so I was comfortable to share the events in my life. We had met for pizza at a local restaurant for the interview and as I reviewed my life up to that point, it was shocking to hear myself talk. It was like the life I had been describing was not my own. It's another person's story of bad luck. The interview forced me to look at my life as a whole, not just a specific time period. Even I began to wonder how I had survived.

The program was attracting interest in the community, and I was being interviewed for newspaper articles and television programs. As I was preparing for an interview, I was told to think of a response to the question of being seen as a local hero. The theory of me being a hero was baffling. I did not see that I had done anything amazing. Yes, I created a program that helps people, but the true heroes are those affected by this devastating illness.

It does not matter how crappy they may feel, my members will get up and come to class. Imagine having a condition where your motivation is gone, multi-tasking becomes challenging, and depression overwhelms you, and don't forget that it is hard for you to even walk. Now, try to commit to a fitness class once a week. Sounds impossible, eh? It is those people that, despite their fear, anger, and pain, will come and share a moment with me. Those are the true heroes. The heroes are also the spouses and partners who suffer through the pain of watching the person that they know so well slowly deteriorate, but continue to stand by their loved ones. The heroes are the Doctors, Nurses, and Surgeons that give their heart and soul to help improve the quality of life for Parkies. I am just a person who saw an opportunity to make a difference and I can only hope that when the day comes that I can no longer do this, that there will be a charismatic, determined person to take my spot.

Due to my medical history, I have always viewed Doctors as mythical creatures, like unicorns. I remember the first time that I saw my surgeon, Dr. Melcer, shopping with his family at the grocery store. I stared at him like I had just seen the white rabbit from "Alice in Wonderland". How could he possibly be shopping at the store amongst us mere mortals? But now that I am working out of a Neurosurgeon's office, it gives the word "Doctor" a whole new meaning. They are just normal people like you and I; one of life's little lessons.

With this gift of working for Dr. Duma, I have had the opportunity to rub elbows with some of the most prestigious Physicians in Southern California. I am able to sneak into their offices and steal a minute of their time with questions about the Parkinson's condition. This has allowed me the advantage of learning and sharing information. If one of my members has a question that I cannot answer, I am able to ask my boss. No appointment necessary. This has been an awesome tool when looking for guest speakers or verifying facts about the latest research.

Another added bonus of launching the program was the amount of people I could reach by getting involved. I began attending and participating in every opportunity to gain information, meet influential people in the community and introduce the resources FNSR had to offer. But this did not come without a cost.

First was the shock of recognizing that places where I had once gotten my support had now begun to view me as a threat. I have always been told that there are politics in everything but I never anticipated to find it in the non-profit world, where helping others was supposed to be the main goal. To my dismay, I noticed that there were boundaries created by the non-profit organizations. Where you lived or what hospital your Physicians were affiliated with, influenced what resources you learned about. I have experienced the constant internal battle that hides behind the community's eyes. With this knowledge, I have dedicated my efforts to the community of Parkinson's by complimenting other programs, not competing.

Secondly, I was now completely absorbed in the Parkinson's condition. I would work with people all day long and then go home and try to find a way to cope with the fact that I had PD. I began to be Mrs. Parkinson's, 24 hours a day. I needed to work towards finding my own balance in life.

I tried to ignore my symptoms and focus on other activities; almost like I was in denial. My parents, Jason and I had signed up for a 5K walk to raise money for a national foundation. It was such a rush to carry signs with the words "Parkinson's disease" capitalized with glitter as we cheered and walked. It was a great chance to raise awareness to hundreds of people. But my Parkinson's had another idea, it was going to act like a Diva and make the event all about her! As we rounded the last loop of the walk, I could feel my body getting tired and each step became a little heavier. I began to get rigid and I could feel a case of Dystonia (Rapture Claw, as my husband calls it) about to hit.

I have to admit, I did think about quitting the second half but I looked around and realized that I was surrounded by family and my husband. I felt safe and knew that if I needed support, they would be there to help. I did not need to pretend that I did not have the illness that I was so passionate about. I needed to embrace the fact that I was so young and energetic, all while coping with PD. It gave me a chance to make a difference. So I took some Sinemet and a drink of water and kept pushing forward. When I finished the 5K, I had a moment where I felt incredibly fortunate. I had used the power of my support system and leaned on my family in my time of need. But you want to know the magic of that day? It was when I recognized that I felt like I was beginning to fall, but they were there to catch me. I was not alone.

I had been surrounded by people who have unimaginable struggles on a daily basis all alone....no family, no husband, and sometimes not even a friend. We become so focused on our own pain that we miss the moments that we need to embrace. There is not a minute in my day that I don't have someone to lean on. I know that when I feel weak, I can look to my family, my friends, or my husband (my rock) and I will find the support I need to keep fighting. For those moments of realization......I am grateful.

In my support groups, I began to emphasis the concept of creating a "PD Wolfpack". This is a group of people including family, friends, medical staff or anyone else that you may rely on to bring you strength in your hour of darkness. My "PD Wolfpack" just gave me the encouragement that I needed to finish my 5K walk. This can also prevent the overload that can be placed on the caring partners of the Parkie, seeing as there are multiple sources of support. I do not like to use the term "Patient and Caregiver." It takes away the fact that at one point, a couple considered themselves married. There were reasons why they fell in love, and experiences that keep them together. The mere fact that a medical illness had disrupted the family does not give us the right to categorize and define the parameters of our loving relationships.

Epilogue:
A Happy Ending on a Roller Coaster

I always loved rodents, and they are life size!
This was at a movie with a friend, a couple weeks after my unexpected surgery in 2011.

As I was writing this memoir in November 2011, I started having strange pelvic pain. I decided to go into the emergency room (ER) at a local hospital just to make sure that there was nothing serious going on. Like my Dad always says, "We hate it when people ask how you are doing, because we never know if in the morning you could be fine, and in the evening, in the hospital." I am starting to see that he was always right, yes Dad, I said it! I went into the ER in the morning and that evening I was being prepped for emergency abdominal surgery.

It was almost ominous the way I got up that morning, showered and packed a bag. I can never foresee what will happen once I get to the hospital, but I know how to prepare. I packed a couple of tank tops, of course with the built-in bra, which allows me to wear that freeing gown that ties in the back and still be suitable to go through radiology for any testing. I always take lip balm, lotion, and big fluffy socks, but the most important item in my bag is "Blue Blankin", discreetly tucked in the bottom of my bag.

I get into my car and try to focus on the road and not the fact that I am driving myself to the hospital, alone. I did not want to affect Jason's classes, so I thought that I would go see if there was anything seriously wrong and save him from the all-consuming experience. My hands grip the steering wheel and I hear the sound of muffled music. I change the song that is playing about every 30 seconds, nothing is soothing. Each note that rings out of my car's speakers is like trying to tolerate nails scratching a chalk board. I finally arrive at the hospital and conveniently pull up to the valet curb. Hey, I live in Orange County, California....what do you expect?!

I am sitting on, shall we call them pleather (a hybrid creation of plastic and leather) covered chairs waiting for my name to be called. The room is detailed with fake plastic plants and a vending machine. I can feel my legs getting slippery from the synthetic furniture. I wonder "How could any person make this experience comfortable?" I could have been lying on a fluffy cloud with a cherub fanning me with a palm leaf while hand feeding me chocolate, it does not take away the fact that I am about to enter into medical hell.

I knew what was happening, but it was the first time that I had gone into the emergency room and been admitted before a test was even completed. My fallopian tube had collected a large amount of fluid and it was pressing against my other vital organs. I know my body extremely well at this point and the pain was familiar. During summer of 2011, I was admitted into the hospital for the same type of pain. Tests revealed that I had collected over a liter of fluid in my fallopian tube. They drained the fluid and placed a tube in my abdomen that could allow my body to expel the liquid. Dr. Lisa Abaid, M.D., who practices gynecological oncology, has been monitoring my "situation" for years. She was not going to let me come in again and just treat the symptom. A CT scan confirmed that my tubes had collected fluid again and the only option at this point was to remove them.

Here is the catch, I have these problems because of a large amount of adhesions in my abdomen causing restrictions to my vital organs, but if we do another surgery we could just create more problems. An adhesion is a band of scar tissue that binds two different parts of tissue together that should remain separate. They may appear as thin sheets of tissue similar to plastic wrap or as thick fibrous bands. Enough with the medical jargon, I was told that my abdominal cavity looks like someone just dumped glue inside me and everything is sticking to itself in funky places. Take that Wikipedia!

I was surprisingly calm. I texted Jason so he could come be with me and called my parents; we all were nervous, but knew that something had to be done. My parents were on speaker phone asking questions and voicing their concerns. Dr. Abaid was nodding her head and responding with ease. I zoned out mentally, I knew we would try to do this Laparoscopically, (which would mean they would make small incisions and use a camera to do the surgery) but that it would ultimately lead to an abdominal surgery. This brought on a rush of emotions and I thought, "What if they perforate my internal pouch? I could be left with a colostomy bag for the rest of my life." I pushed any negative thoughts from my head and focused on the goal.

I truly believe that your body has a protection mechanism that allows you to push traumatic events out of your mind. I know that medication comes into play, but the next five days are blurry. Dr. Abaid, being an awesome Surgeon, was able to remove both tubes, but I did have my tummy cut into again. Jason was with me every night in the hospital, sleeping on the couch. I was not alone. Cards and flowers began to pour into our home. The support from my family and friends kept me strong. I was Allison and if anyone could do this, it was me. Besides, at the rate I am going, I am running out of body parts that they can remove!

The following days after leaving the hospital are always the worst. I had been getting pain and nausea medication every few hours through an IV for days, but now I was home. As I was coming off all the drugs and trying to pull myself together, I had to cancel some of my classes and groups. I thought it was best to be honest and let my members know that I had a setback. The energy from those concerned helped me stay focused on healing. Trying to stay positive was not easy, but then I realized the amount of people that sent emails and cards had just reaffirmed my ultimate goal had been achieved; my program had encouraged strangers to come together to share their pain and in return our friendship became support for each other. Boy did I feel the love!

True to character, my surgery did not go as planned. Three days out of the hospital, I got a bowel obstruction. I did not know how I could stay strong and go back to the hospital, but I did not have a choice!

I spent 6 more days in the hospital on bowel rest. I had a picc line placed in my arm and I was being fed TPN (total I.V. nutrition...no chips and sips here) to ensure I got all my nutrients needed to stay healthy. It was ironic that this happened as I was writing my book. It was just like my body was saying, "Oh, how cute are you! You thought you could go a year without being in the hospital." Something else that had been emotionally draining was the realization that I would not be able to have a child seeing as my tubes had to be removed. Deep down inside I knew that I wouldn't be getting pregnant in my lifetime, but I was faced with the cold reality that I physically could not. I am so grateful that my brother Todd and his wife Beth have two beautiful children. I get the experience of being the cool aunt who buys the best gifts!

People ask me, "Where do you get your strength to deal with all of your health challenges?" I began to think about that question. Where does my drive come from? How can I take something so horrible, but somehow make it pleasant? Why have I never given up hope? When my mother is bragging about me, she tells people that one thing that has impressed her is my ability to look for that other door, when one closes.

Possibly my strength comes from something deep within me. My father loves genealogy and has spent years collecting data. He researches our family tree, hoping to get a glimpse of how we have become the people we are today. Dad tells me stories of the strength and determination of our ancestors who came over on the Mayflower and fought in the Revolutionary War. Maybe that explains how I have the go-power to get up each morning to face down Parkinson's, or maybe it is something more.

As you read this book, you might be thinking, "What can this girl be grateful for?" or my favorite, "If you would have known that your life would turn out this way..." My response to these questions is, "Of course I wish that I could have lived a normal life, free of medical illness and emotional torment, but I wouldn't know the amazing people that are a part of my life now. I would have not had the opportunity to see the potential I had inside me and I would have not become the person I am today."

The truth of the matter is, when you are forced to sit in this pain and let it completely absorb your very existence, you have the luxury of choice. Now, I know what you are saying, "Who chooses to get ill?" I agree with that, but I did have control over how I reacted. I could have decided to curl up into a ball, move back into my parents' house and give up on life, but I didn't. I cannot change what has happened, but I do have control over how I react to it.

When I am speaking to a group of Parkies, my favorite question to ask the audience is, "What are you grateful for in your life because you got Parkinson's disease?" I usually get confused or shocked expressions. It is grueling to think about the reverse when you are in pain-emotional, or physical. I have just asked you to be optimistic when, for the last days, months or even years, you have been knocked to the ground by your new diagnosis. Whether you can see it, or choose to admit it, the challenge that you are faced with today has brought an element into your life that is positive.

I am thankful that I was diagnosed with Cancer. Being close to death forced me to feel the pain of being alone. I don't wait to tell my loved ones exactly how much I love them or my friends how important they are to me. Have you ever thought, "Where did the year go?" Bingo! Time does not stop, and one day you will realize you are running out of it. Just like Thomas Jefferson said, "Never put off till tomorrow what you can do today." This quote reminds me that there might not be a tomorrow. How do you want to spend the remaining time you have in this world?

I understand that my symptoms are different every day and my "on" time is limited. This requires me to be choosy as to "who" or "what" I spend my energy on. If you are not significant to me, I am not going to give you my precious time. I cannot let meaningless conflicts or shady people take space in my head. I will not waste a minute of my valuable time worrying about things that I cannot change.

I am grateful for the multitude of medical procedures I have been through because I know what pain is and how it can alter your very existence. I am now more understanding and patient when I am around people who are angry or sad because the truth is, I have no clue as to what is going on in their life. Sometimes it can feel like we are all alone in this world, bumping into each other, only worried about ourselves. But we have one thing in common, we have all experienced pain. Now if I could only find a way to cure world hunger...

all in good time!

I am appreciative for the transformation in my marriage since Mrs. Parkinson's came knocking on my door, or shall I say brain. I learned to be vulnerable and to trust my husband. This last year of my life has brought us to a new level of understanding. I know that he will be there for me when I am weak. I can trust that he will be my rock when emotionally I cannot find the strength to remain positive as my body slowly deteriorates. In my pain, I have found someone who is not afraid to stand beside me during the unknown. Thank you Parkinson's....you have humbled me.

It does not matter if our experiences are the same. You will never find a life identical to your own. If you have someone in your life that is facing medical a challenge, go to them. Many people will abandon loved ones in their time of need out of fear of not knowing what to say. This is only due to their fear of mortality. If it could happen to Allison, then maybe it can happen to me. You don't have to fix them. Just be present in the one thing that you two are sharing...human pain. I am not contagious. We are not contagious. I am not infecting anyone and I promise that if you hug me, you will not get sick.

I wish that I can find a way to take a smidgen of someone's pain away. If my life's work can help one person, then I have found the meaning of my journey. If I had a magic wand, I would "poof" and make disease disappear. But unfortunately my "poofer" is not working right now, so my only hope is that this book may bring you a little closer to my world. I have shared a glimpse of my life with you. What you take from it, is up to you.

I am not sure how those close to me will handle the slow deterioration of my body and spirit. I believe deep down inside that I will be alright. I hope that I can live a life that would make my parents proud. And when I am gone, I hope that I have changed the lives of many, and people will say, "I am honored to have been a part of Allison's life." But it is not only within me, a single person with an innate passion; it is within all of us. The meaning of our lives is determined by the experiences that have shaped us. Be inspired. Find what you stand for and fight. It does not matter what is motivating you, it will be different for each of us. Seek opportunities to come together and share our lives, because we are only stronger in numbers. We can find love, support, and strength in pain merely by being in each other's presence. May you find health, happiness, and inspiration, but if that is hard to imagine at this time, may hope find you.

My beautiful family and my Dad's awesome mustache.

Luau in the dead of winter in Colorado, yes, my family was crazy.

Feeling safe and secure with Dad and *Blue Blankin*.

My Dad and I are spending some quality time on the floor. I think this is one of the only pictures of *Blue Blakin* before she became a ball of yarn.

1981 at Disneyland. I think I have my Dad's mustache; it was growing in quite nicely.

My lemonade stand guinea pig, sugar. I now know that you can't walk your pig, but it seemed like a good idea at the time.

Pueblo County High Marching Band. After leaving the squad, I had to find a new passion. Some of my favorite memories happened during my years in band.

Freshman year in High School.
I had just begun to get joint pain that year.

The best way to get warm, put your booty by the heater.

My brother Todd and Beth's wedding, a beautiful event.

Doc, Wyatt and I enjoying the roses.

My papa and parents at my celebration from Graduate School.

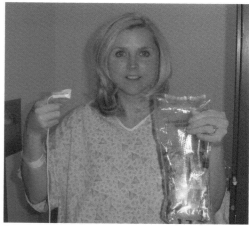

My lovely hospital gown and my saline cocktail.

Picking a dinosaur's nose. I have many talents.

Graduation with my best friend, Casie Sullivan.

Marine Corp Ball, I still get butterflies seeing Jason in his dress blues.

At Santa Ana Court House getting hitched! December 18th, 2008.

The beginning of two amazing couples. My roommate, Casey and her boyfriend Anthony Klein, out to dinner with Jason and me.

Working at Phoenix House,
promoting my fitness program.

Our wedding reception in June 2009.
We both look smokin' hot!

The best remedy for healing from medical procedures, comfy clothes and my
doggie nurse, Crash.

118

Have you ever seen a dog laugh?
Bella and I can't stop giggling.

October 2010 Jason and my family walking the Long Beach 5K
to raise Parkinson's awareness. The same month I launched my program
Parkinson's in Balance.

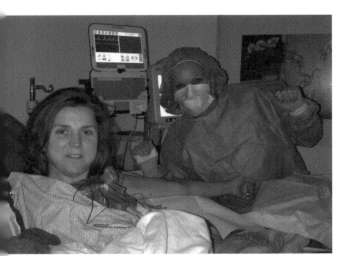

My emergency surgery in November 2011, my new red hairdo
helped get me through the tough times!

Jason and I at FNSR's first fundraiser at the Balboa Bay Club in Newport Beach.

Christopher Duma, MD, FACS

Board-certified neurosurgeon specialist Christopher Duma, MD, FACS, serves as Chair of the Foundation for Neurosciences, Stroke and Recovery, and remains active in Orange County's medical community as Medical Director of Brain and Spine Surgeons of OC and Medical Director of the Brain Tumor Program at Hoag Memorial Hospital Presbyterian in Newport Beach, California. He also serves as Assistant Clinical Professor of Neurosurgery at the University of California, Irvine's School of Medicine as well as Director of Radiosurgery for UCI Medical Center's Department of Neurosurgery residency training program.

Dr. Duma received his general neurosurgical training at Georgetown University Hospital in Washington, D.C., followed by a fellowship at the University of Pittsburgh Medical Center Presbyterian in Gamma Knife radiosurgery and stereotactic and functional neurosurgery. He has been involved in medical research since his undergraduate education, beginning at the Cornell University School of Medicine's Department of Neuropharmacology and continuing on through his graduate years at Memorial Sloan-Kettering Cancer Center's Department of Neurology Pain Service.

In 2004, Dr. Duma, MD founded The Foundation for Neurosciences, Stroke and Recovery to provide outreach and assistance to patients with movement disorders. Dr. Duma resides in Newport Beach, California with his wife, Jessica, and their three children. His outside interests include playing piano/keyboards, wine tasting and relaxing in Cape Cod, Massachusetts, with his family. To contact Dr. Duma please call 949-642-6787 and his address is: 3900 West Coast Highway, Suite 300 Newport Beach, CA 92663.

Allison Smith-Conway, MA, NASM-CPT

We all find some cause to support at one time or another, but with Allison Smith-Conway, the causes seem to find her. Allison was diagnosed with Colon Cancer at the age of 24 and went through 13 surgeries within three years due to complications. After fighting for her life in her 20's, she is now fighting another chronic disease, Parkinson's disease, which she was diagnosed with at the age of 32.

Despite all this, Allison, 34, looks healthy and has the energy of an athlete. Her motto is that any dilemma "doesn't need to be a negative experience." After completing her Deep Brain Stimulation surgeries, and before the 34 staples in her head were removed, she knew the path of her life was about to change. She made her diagnosis public and began searching for ways that she could bring hope to the community of which she is now a part. Parkinson's disease can be very aggressive and can cause major problems in future years, such as tremor, loss of mobility, cognitive and speech issues.

Seeing the need for support in the lives of those affected by debilitating illness, Allison uses her knowledge and strength to help people that face the challenges that come with this disease. With her unique insight, she created a program called Parkinson's in Balance which brings individual/family psychotherapy, support groups, community events, and fitness classes to those with Parkinson's. All services are offered at no cost. Allison states "Parkinson's disease has no idea what I am capable of, and as long as there is air in my rigid body, I will seek out opportunities to weaken the disease and give hope to its victims."

Allison Smith-Conway holds a Master's degree in Marital and Family Therapy with an emphasis on Health and Fitness. Allison is a personal trainer certified through National Academy of Sports Medicine (NASM), holding certifications in Sports Performance and Corrective exercise. As part of Allison's commitment to community education and awareness, she is available to speak to groups about the emotional aspects of Parkinson's disease, creating your *PD wolfpack*, and other resources offered by her program. For more information about classes and workshops led by Allison, such as "Parkies and Partners" or *Parkinson's in Balance* "Fun with Fitness," please call her at **(866) 232-2526 x2** or email her at **allison@parkinsonsinbalance.net.**

3

Foundation for Neurosciences Stroke and Recovery (FNSR) is a non-profit organization, which was established in 2004 and is based in Southern California. With the passion to enhance the lives of individuals and families who have been affected by neurological ailments, our mission is to touch lives by providing education, support groups, fitness classes, psychotherapy, and community outreach programs.

Foundation for Neuroscience, Stroke and Recovery will be growing in the next few years, with plans for the addition of Stoke and Brain Tumor programs. Our ability to maintain these programs and offer resources at no cost to the community relies on the generosity of its donors. Please visit our website for more information and or to donate.

www.fnsroc.org

You may also reach us at:
FNSR
P.O. Box 7617
Laguna Niguel, CA 92677
(866) 232-2526

Appendix

Books:

- Parkinson's disease: Diagnosis and Clinical Management, by Stewart A. Factor and William J. Weiner

- Life with a Battery-Operated Brain: A patient's guide to Deep Brain Stimulation surgery for Parkinson's disease, by Jackie Hunt Christensen

- What your Doctor may not tell you about Parkinson's disease: A Holistic program for Optimal Wellness, by Jill Marajama-Lyons, M.D. and Mary Shomon.

Websites:

- http://www.michaeljfox.org

- http://davisphinneyfoundation.org

- http://en.wikipedia.org/wiki/Parkinson's_disease

- http://www.webmd.com/parkinsons-disease/parkinsons-overview

- http://www.stlapda.org/content/pdfs/Young%20Parkinson%20Handbook.pdf

CPSIA information can be obtained
at www.ICGtesting.com
Printed in the USA
270002LV00001B

9781468549058